BONSAI ART
EUROPE 1

First published in 1998 by **Moyogi Books**
an imprint of Colin Lewis & Associates
PO box 317, West Byfleet, Surrey KT14 6YG

ISBN 0 9532287 0 3

Colour reproduction by Rivermead Design
Printed in Italy

**The royalties from the sale of this book
will be donated to the European Bonsai
Association**

Acknowledgments

TRANSLATION
Thanks are due to the following for undertaking
the difficult task of translating the texts:

Victoria Bruton; Karola Cressati; Krista Leach;
Stéphane & Corinne Noireau; Yasushi Oonuma;
Sophie Pike; Laurence Pintaurault; Erwin
Verheyen.

PHOTOGRAPHY
The work of the following photographers is
reproduced on the pages indicated.

Willy & An Evenepoel: 54>61. **Mariano
Fagiani:** 18>29. **Anel Fernández:** 115, 116,
122>125. **Chris Gordon:** 32, 38>41. **Bill Jordan:**
front cover, 126>137. **Jose Pérez:** 114, 119. **Helmut Rüger:** 79, 86>89. All other photographs
were taken by the authors.

The publisher is also grateful to the eleven artists
who generously contributed to this edition, and
would also like to thank the following for their
help and support: Malcolm Hughes; Rene Vantilt;
Michel Sacal; Michel Vitrat; Maria Makris; Jerry
Day; Marco Invernizzi.

BONSAI ART
EUROPE 1

IN AID OF
THE EUROPEAN
BONSAI ASSOCIATION

moyogi
BOOKS

Bonsai Art Europe

During the last two decades the art of bonsai has developed at a rapid pace throughout the western world – nowhere more so than in Europe.

Its wide diversity of cultures and natural landscapes, its rich and varied artistic heritage and the ever-increasing co-operation between nations and individuals, have combined to form a dynamic new approach. Creativity, imagination and the willingness to experiment are the hallmarks of European bonsai.

Whilst retaining traditional values, European artists are beginning to challenge the traditional frontiers of bonsai art. With a new-found confidence in their skills and judgement, they are no longer reluctant to make their own artistic statements.

This book is the first to serve as a showcase for some of the finest bonsai artists Europe has to offer. The distinctive style of each artist, as depicted in the portraits of their works, will provide enthusiasts in all parts of the world with a rich source of inspiration. Their thoughts, expressed in the accompanying texts, will stimulate others to formulate their own ideas and, hopefully, to take further steps forward in the development of this unique and most compelling artistic discipline.

Sincere thanks are due to all those who have contributed to this book – not only for sharing with us their thoughts and images, but also for their generosity in donating their royalties to the European Bonsai Association.

Negli ultimi vent'anni l'arte di bonsai si è sviluppata rapidamente in tutto il mondo occidentale e soprattutto in Europa.

Le sue grandi diversità culturali e naturali ed il suo ricco e vario patrimonio artistico insieme alla sempre più crescente collaborazione tra nazioni ed individui hanno creato un nuovo approccio dinamico. La creatività, l'immaginazione e la disponibilità di sperimentare sono diventati il marchio del bonsai Europeo.

Mentre conservano i loro valori tradizionali, gli artisti di bonsai Europei cominciano a sfidare le barriere tradizionali dell'arte bonsai. Insieme ad una fiducia innovativa nelle loro capacità e giudizio non hanno più paura di dichiarare le loro nozioni artistiche.

Questo libro serve da vetrina per alcuni dei migliori artisti in Europa. Lo stile individuale di ogni artista, mostrato nelle descrizioni delle loro opere, fornirà una fonte ricca di ispirazione a tutti i bonsaisti mondiali.

I loro pensieri, espressi nei testi di accompagnamento, stimoleranno l'immaginazione di molti altri e, speriamo, di avanzare ulteriormente verso lo sviluppo di questa unica ed affascinante disciplina artistica.

Dei ringraziamenti sinceri sono dovuti a tutte le persone che hanno contribuito a questo libro, non soltanto per aver condiviso con noi i loro pensieri ed immagini ma anche per la loro generosità nel donare le royalties alla European Bonsai Association.

Durante las dos últimas décadas, el arte de bonsai ha desarrollado de una manera muy rápida a través del mundo occidental; sobre todo en Europa.

Su amplia diversidad de culturas y paisajes naturales, su rica y variada historia cultual y artistíca, la continua cooperación entre las diferentes naciones e individuos, se han fundido hasta crear una forma fresca y dinámica de introducción. Creatividad, imaginación, y la voluntad de experimentar, son las caracteristícas principales del bonsai europeo.

Mientras que preservan sus valores tradicionales, los artistas europeos están iniciando un nuevo reto en las barreras tradicionales del arte de bonsai. Con una nueva seguridad en su habilidad y juicio, ya no existe esa timided al anunciar sus propios criterios.

Este libro es el primero que sirve como archivo de los mejores artistas, que Europa tiene que ofrecer. El estilo distintivo de cada artista, representado en cada uno de los siguientes artículos sobre su trabajo, proporcionan una rica fuente de inspiración para entusiastas de cualquier rincón del mundo. Sus pensamientos, expresados en los textos siguientes estimularán a otros para así formular ellos mismos sus propias ideas, y posiblemente para dar nuevos pasos en el desarrollo de esta disciplina artística.

Quisiera por último dar sinceramente las gracias a todos aquellos que han contribuido a este libro, no solamente por compartir con nosotros sus pensamientos e imágenes, sino además por su generosidad al donar las ganancias de este trabajo, a La Asociación Europea de Bonsai.

Pendant les vingts dernières années, l'art bonsaï s'est développé rapidement à travers tout l'occident et surtout en Europe.

Sa grande diversité de cultures, de paysages naturels, son héritage artistique riche et varié, et la coopération toujours plus grande entre les nations et les hommes produisent une nouvelle approche très dynamique. La créativité, l'imagination et le désir d'expérimenter sont les caractéristiques du bonsaï Européen.

Tout en conservant les valeurs traditionnelles, les artistes Européens commencent à remettre en question les frontières traditionnelles de l'art bonsaï. Sûrs de leur savoir faire et de leur jugement récemment acquis, ils n'hésitent plus à imposer leurs propres formulations artistiques.

Ce livre est le premier à servir de vitrine à plusieurs des meilleurs artistes à bonsaï Européens. Le style caractéristique de chaque artiste, démontré par son travail, sera pour les amateurs de bonsaï du monde entier, une riche source d'inspiration. Leurs pensées, exprimées dans les textes suivants, stimuleront les lecteurs à formuler leurs idées propres, et nous espérons, à une démarche qui contribuera au dévelopement de cette discipline artistique irrésistible, unique.

Nos remerciements sincères à tous ceux qui ont contribué à ce livre - non seulement pour avoir partagé leurs pensées et leurs image avec nous, mais aussi pour leur générosité en donnant leurs droits d'auteurs à l'Association Européenne de Bonsaï.

Während der letzten zwei Jahrzehnte hat sich die Nonsaikunst sehr schnell in der westlichen Welt entwickelt - nirgendwo mehr als in Europa.

Europas große Vielfalt an Kulturen und natürlichen Landschaften, sein reiches und mannigfaltiges künstlerisches Erbe und die stets wachsende Zusammenarbeit von Nationen und Individualisten haben sich zu einer neuen, dynamischen Einstellung vereint. Kreativität, Vorstellungskraft und Experimentierwille sind Kennzeichen europäischer Bonsai.

Während sie an traditionellen Werten festhalten, fangen die europäischen Künstler an, die traditionellen Grenzen der Bonsaikunst herauszufordern. Mit einem neu gefundenen Vertrauen in ihre Urteilskraft, sind sie nicht länger abgeneigt, ihre eigenen künstlerischen Aussagen zu machen. Dieses Buch ist das erste, das als Schaukasten für einige der besten Bonsaikünstler, die Europa zu bieten hat, dient.

Der kennzeichnende Stil eines jeden Künstlers, so wie er in den Porträts ihrer Werke geschildert wird, wird Liebhaber in allen Teilen der Welt mit einer reichen Quelle der Inspiration versorgen. Die Gedanken der Künstler, ausgedrückt in den begleitenden Texten, wird andere dazu stimulieren, ihre eigenen Ideen zu formulieren und hoffentlich dazu bringen, weitere Schritte zu Entwicklung dieser einzigartigen und überwältigenden Kunstdisziplin zu machen.

Herzlicher Dank gebührt allen, die zu diesem Buch beigetragen haben - nicht nur weil sie mit uns ihre Gedanken und Ideen geteilt haben, sondern auch dafür, daß sie ihre Tantiemen der European Bonsai Association geschenkt haben.

HOLLAND

Farrand Bloch

Farrand Bloch was born in Holland in March 1965, and discovered bonsai via his interest in Japanese gardens and art. He first began attending bonsai workshops at the age of 20 and spent several years studying with Hotsumi Terakawa.

In 1992, Farrand travelled to Japan, where he studied at Shigeo Kuroso's bonsai garden in Omiya. On returning to Holland, he continued his studies by attending classes with Yuji Yoshimura and Suchin Ee. He also developed a strong interest in bonsai ceramics and took lessons from the ceramist Jassu Kaneko.

In the spring of 1993, Farrand opened his own bonsai studio and began giving lessons and workshops a year later. He rapidly developed his own style which gained him invitations to teach in several European countries including Italy, Germany, the United Kingdom, Belgium and Denmark, as well as his native Holland.

Farrand Bloch has been a full-time bonsai artist since 1995 and considers his major international breakthrough was at the 1995 summer convention at Greenwood bonsai studio in Nottingham, England. Following this, he was invited to be the main international teacher at the annual convention in Melville, New York. After the convention he remained in the USA to conduct demonstrations and workshops at a number of clubs, as well as for several private American collectors.

Farrand Bloch has written numerous articles for international magazines, covering al aspects of bonsai art and techniques. He is scheduled to teach at the BCI International Convention to be held in Puerto Rico, South America in 1998.

Farrand Bloch è nato in Olanda nel marzo del 1965 e ha scoperto il bonsai tramite il suo interesse per i giardini e l'arte giapponese. A ventanni ha inziato a frequentare una scuola di bonsai, studiando inoltre sotto la guida di Hotsumi Terakawa.

Nel 1992 Farrand si è recato in Giappone dove ha lavorato nel giardino bonsai di Shigeo Kuroso in Omya. Al rientro in Olanda ha continuato i suoi studi, frequentando corsi con Yuji Yoshimura e Suchin Ee. Ha sviluppato una forte interesse per le ceramiche bonsai studiandone le tecniche dal ceramista Jassu Kaneko.

Nella primavera del 1993 Farrand ha aperto un suo studio bonsai, iniziando a tenere lezioni e dimostrazioni un'anno dopo. Il suo stile molto personale lo ha portato a insegnare in diversi paesi europei quali Italia, la Germania, l'Inghilterra, il Belgio e la Danimarca nonchè nella sua nativa Olanda.

Farrand Bloch è un'artista bonsai a tempo pieno dal 1995 e ritiene che il culmine della sua carriera sia arrivato durante il convego d'estate allo Studio bonsai di Greenwood nel 1995 a Nottingham, Inghilterra. E` stato invitato inoltre al convengo di Melville, New York come dimostratore più importante. Dopo il convegno è rimasto negli USA per tenere parecchie dimostrazioni nei Club nonchè per curare delle collezioni private americane.

Farrand Bloch ha scritto numerosi articoli per riviste internazionali, parlando di arte come di tecnica bonsai. Sarà uno dei dimostratori ufficiali al convegno della BCI International che si terrà a Puerto Rico, in Sud America nel 1998.

Taxus cuspidata

70cm

165 years / jahre / anni / ans / años

Japan

Walsall Studio

◀ *'White Wings'*
Chamaecyparis obtusa nana 'gracilis'
⌃⌄ 60cm
35 years / jahre / anni / ans / años
Holland
⌷ Tokoname

Farrand Bloch nació en Holanda en Marzo de 1965 y descubrió bonsai por medio de su interés en la jardinería y el arte japonés. A la edad de veinte años comenzó a acudir a talleres de bonsai además de estudiar durante varios años con Hotsumi Terakawa.

En 1992, Farrand viajó a Japón, donde estudió en el jardín de bonsai de Shige Kuroso en Omiya. A su regreso a Holanda, continuó sus estudios acudiendo a las clases de Yuri Yoshimua y Sushin Ee. Contiguamente empezó a surgirle un gran interés en las cerámicas de bonsai y tomó lecciones con el ceramista Jassu Kaneko.

En la primavera de 1993, Farrand inaguró su propio estudio de bonsai y empezó a dar clases y demostraciones un año más tarde. Rapidamente desarrolló su propio estilo por el que obtuvo invitaciones para dar lecciones en varios paises europeos como Italia, Alemania, Gran Bretana, Bélgica y Dinamarca además de su Holanda natal.

Farrand Bloch se ha dedicado plenamente al arte de bonsai desde 1995 y considera la convención del verano de ese mismo año sostenida en el estudio de bonsai de Greenwood en Nottingham, Inglaterra, la oportunidad clave para su reconocimiento a nivel internacional Seguidamente, fué honrado con una invitación para ejercer como profesor internacional principal en la convención anual de Melville, de Nueva York. Posteriormente permaneció en América donde condujo demostraciones y talleres para un gran número de clubs y coleccionistas privados.

Farrand Bloch ha escrito diversos articulos para revistas internacionales, cubriendo aspectos del arte del bonsai y sus técnicas. Está previsto que impartirá clases en la Convención Internacional BCI que se celebrará en Puerto Rico en 1998.

Farrand Bloch est né en Hollande en Mars 1965. Il découvrit les bonsaïs grâce à son intérêt pour les jardins Japonais et l'art. Il assista à ses premiers ateliers de bonsaï à 20 ans et passa plusieures années à étudier avec Hotsumi Terakawa.

En 1992, Farrand partit pour le Japon où il étudia aux jardins de bonsaï de Shigeo Kuroso à Omiya. Quand il revint en Hollande, il continua ses études en suivant des cours menés par Yuji Yoshimura et Suchin Ee. Il développa aussi un fort intérêt pour les coupes à bonsaï en céramique et prit des cours avec le potier Jassu Kaneko.

Au printemps 1993, Farrand ouvrit son propre atelier de bonsaïs. Il commença à donner des cours et un an après organisa des ateliers. Il développa rapidement son propre style, ce qui lui permit d'être invité à enseigner dans plusieurs pays d'Europe dont l'Italie, l'Allemagne, le Royaume Uni, la Belgique, le Danemark et aussi sa Hollande natale.

A partir de 1995, Farrand Bloch devint un artiste en bonsaï professionnel. D'après lui, sa percée internationale eut lieu à une convention, en été 1995, à l'atelier de bonsaï de Greenwood, à Nottingham, en Angleterre. Après, on l'invita à devenir l'enseignant international principal à la convention annuelle de Melville, à New York. Après la convention, il resta aux Etats-Unis pour diriger des démonstrations et des ateliers dans plusieurs clubs ainsi que pour plusieurs collectionneurs privés Americains.

Farrand Bloch a écrit un grand nombre d'articles pour des magazines internationaux, traitant de tous les aspects de l'art et des techniques liés aux bonsaïs. Il projette d'enseigner à la convention internationale du BCI qui aura lieu à Porto Rico, en Amérique du Sud en 1998.

Farrand Bloch wurde im März 1965 in Holland geboren. Er entdeckte Bonsai durch sein Interesse an japanischen Gärten und japanischer Kunst. Seine werten Workshops besuchte er als er zwanzig war und lernte viele Jahre bei Hotsumi Terakawa.

1992 reiste Farrand nach Japan, wo er im Bonsaigarten von Shigeo Kuroso in Omiya Studierte. Nach Holland zurückgekehrt, vertiefte er seine Studien, indem er bei Yuji Yoshimura und Suchin Ee in die Schule ging. Er entwickelte auch ein starkes Interesse für Bonsaikeramik und nahm Unterricht bei dem Keramiker Jassu Kaneko.

Im Frühjar 1993 eröffnete Farrand sein eigenes Bonsaistudio und begann ein Jahr später damit, selbst Unterricht und Workshops zu geben. Sehr schnell entwickelte er seinen eigenen Stil, was ihm Einladungen zum Unterrichten in verschiedenen europäischen Ländern wie z.B. Italien, Deutschland, Großbritannien, Belgien, Dänemark sowie in seinem Heimatland Holland, einbrachten.

Seit 1995 ist Farrand Bloch professioneller Bonsaikünstler. Er selbst meint, sein großer internationaler Durchbruch war im gleichen Jahr beim Sommerkongreß im Greenwood - Bonsaistudio in Nottingham, England. Danach wurde er als internationaler Hauptdemonstrator zum Jahreskongreß nach Melville, New York, eingeladen. Nach dem Kongreß blieb er in den Vereinigten Staaten, um bei vielen Clubs und bei vielen privaten amerikanischen Sammlern Demonstrationen und Workshops zu halten.

Farrand Bloch hat viele Artikel für internationale Magazine über die Aspekte der Bonsaikunst und - Technik geschrieben. Er ist zum Kongreß der BCI (Bonsai Clubs International) 1998 in Puerto Rico in Südamerika als Lehrer eingeladen.

Farrand Bloch
J.v. Stolberglaan 26,
2252 KA Voorschoten, Holland
Tel: +31 (0)71-561 70 99
Fax: +31 (0)71-561 30 49

Farrand Bloch

IN SEARCH OF A DIFFERENT STYLE

When I started learning bonsai, my teachers taught me, apart from watering, pruning and wiring, that bonsai is an art form in its own right. I learned that a tree can express moods comparable to human emotions. Although a tree is like stone to a sculptor it should express its mood or emotion without losing the concept of bonsai.

As I mastered bonsai techniques I was able to make classically styled bonsai, but it was not satisfying for me. Of course, one can always improve oneself, but I was searching for a personal approach. Questions like: "What makes bonsai art?", "Is bonsai art?" and "What are the boundaries of bonsai as an art?" racked my brain. This is how I started on the long path of developing my own style and looking around for new sources of inspiration.

In the mountains I am inspired by the way nature 'styles' trees. But in Holland there is no real nature nearby – the Dutch landscape is very rational and functional. I noticed that the landscape in Japan is similar, apart from in the mountains. There is little space and direct contact with the wilderness is not possible. So miniaturising nature via bonsai seems logical. It is a reminder of real nature in a stylised form.

Only when bonsai is isolated from nature does it achieve its highest artistic significance. The tokanoma is in ideal place. In the tokanoma bonsai is isolated from extraneous distractions, so that one can concentrate on the displayed tree – a tree styled according to man-made aesthetics. Plain nature is probably too strong and overwhelming to be understood, and needs to be simplified, becoming more and more abstract. Being aware of this, I began to realise that the combination of abstraction and aesthetic principles are key elements in this art form.

Modern ikebana, where abstraction is also vital, has a very open approach to styling. Here the artist works with flowers, branches, pieces of wood etc., like a true

ALLA RICERCA DI UNO STILE DIVERSO

Quando iniziai a studiare bonsai, i miei maestri mi insegnarono oltre all'annaffiatura, alla potatura e alla legatura con il filo, che il bonsai è fondamentalmente una forma d'arte. Ho imparato che un albero può esprimere umori comparabili a quelli umani. Anche se un albero è come la pietra per un scultore, dovrà esprimere il suo umore ed le sue emozioni senza perdere il concetto di bonsai.

Mentre imparavo le tecniche lavorando il bonsai nello stile classico non mi sentivo completamente appagato. Senz'altro ognuno può sempre migliorarsi ma stavo cercando in particolar modo un'approccio personale. Mi chiedevo 'Che fà del bonsai un'arte?', 'Il Bonsai è un'arte vera e propria?' e 'Quali sono i limiti per bonsai come arte?'. E' così iniziai il lungo cammino di sviluppo del mio stile alla ricerca di nuovi fonti d'ispirazione.

In montagna sono ispirato dal modo in cui la natura modella gli alberi. Non esiste una vera natura in Olanda, il paesaggio Olandese è molto razionale e funzionale, simile in alcuni aspetti a quello giapponese, tranne che per le zone montagnose. C'è poco spazio ed il contatto diretto con il selvaggio non è possibile, pertanto rimpicciollire lanatura tramite il bonsai sembra molto logico; il bonsai diventa un'idea di natura in una forma stilizzata.

Soltanto quando il bonsai è isolato dalla natura che il suo significato più vero emerge. Il tokonoma è un posto ideale. Nel tokonoma il bonsai è isolato da distrazioni esterne in modo che ognuno si possa concentrare sull'albero esposto, un'albero modellato secondo l'estetica dell'uomo. La semplice natura è probabilmente troppo forte e sorprendente per essere compresa ed ha bisogno di essere semplificata e astratta. Rendendomi conto di ciò mi sono accorto che la combinazione di astrattismo e principi estetici sono gli elementi chiave in questa forma d'arte.

L'Ikebana moderna, dove l'astrazione è

EN BUSCA DE UN ESTILO DIFERENTE

Cuando empezé a aprender el bonsai, mis profesores me enseñaron, a parte del riego, la poda y el alambrado, que el bonsai es un arte por mérito propio. Aprendí que un árbol puede expresar diferentes aspectos similares al estado emocional humano. Aunque un árbol sea como una piedra, para un escultor debe de expresar su carácter y sentimiento sin perder el concepto de bonsai.

Una vez dominadas las técnicas de bonsai ya era capaz de realizar el bonsai de estilo clásico, pero esto no era suficiente para mí. Por supuesto que uno siempre puede superarse a sí mismo, pero mí busqueda era de tipo personal. Preguntas como: '¿Qué es lo que convierte bonsai en un arte?', '¿Es el bonsai un arte?' y '¿Cual son sus límites como tal?' inquietaban mi mente. Fue así como comenzó el largo camino de crear mi propio estilo y buscar a su vez nuevas fuentes de inspiración.

En las montañas fuí inspirado por la formaen que la naturaleza 'estiliza' los árboles. Sin embargo en Holanda no existe un medio ambiente silvestre – el terreno holandés es muy racional y funcional. Pude comprobar que el paisaje en Japón era similar, con la excepción de las montañas. El espacio es muy limitado y el contacto directo con la flora silvestre es imposible.La miniaturización de la naturaleza por medio del bonsai parecía lógica. Es la reminiscencia de la naturaleza de una forma estilizada.

Solamente cuando el bonsai está aislado de la naturaleza consigue su más alto significado artístico. El tokonoma es el lugar ideal. En el tokonoma el bonsai está aislado completamente de distracciones externas, por lo tanto se puede uno concentrar en el árbol allí expuesto – árbol que esta estilizado desde el punto de vista estético de un ser humano. La naturaleza es posiblemente demasiado fuerte y arrolladora para poder ser comprendida, y necesita por lo tanto ser simplificada, para conseguir ser a su vez más abstracta. Consciente de esto, comencé a darme cuenta que la combinación de los principios abstracto-estéticos, son los ele-

A LA RECHERCHE D'UN AUTRE STYLE

Quand j'ai commencé à étudier les bonsaïs, mes enseignants m'apprirent non seulement comment arroser, élaguer et ligaturer mais aussi à apprécier les bonsaïs comme des oeuvres d'art. J'appris qu'un arbre peut exprimer des états d'âme comparables aux émotions humaines. Un arbre est comme une pierre pour un sculpteur. Il exprime son humeur et ses émotions sans pour cela s'éloigner du concept de l'art du bonsaï.

Quand je maitrisais enfin différentes techniques de bonsaï, je devins capable de créer des bonsaïs stylisés suivant les formes classiques, mais rapidement, cela ne me satisfit plus. Bien sûr, j'aurais pu continuer à améliorer ma technique, mais je cherchais à développer un style plus personnel. Je me creusais la tête avec des questions comme: «Qu'est ce que l'art bonsaï?», «Les bonsaïs sont-ils des oeuvres d'art?», «Quelles sont les limites de l'art bonsaï.» C'est ainsi que j'ai commencé à développer mon propre style, et à chercher de nouvelles sources d'inspiration.

A la montagne, la façon dont la nature «stylise» les arbres m'inspire. Mais en Hollande, il n'y a pas de vraie nature a proximité – le paysage Hollandais est rationnel et fonctionnel. Au japon, le paysage est pareil, sauf dans les montagnes. L'espace est restreint et un contact direct avec la nature est impossible. Dans ce contexte, miniaturiser la nature devient logique. C'est une façon de représenter la nature de façon stylisée.

Un bonsaï doit être isolé de la nature pour réaliser toute sa portée artistique. Le Tokonoma est le lieu idéal. Dans le Tokonoma, le bonsaï est isolé de toute distractions superflues, ainsi, on peut se concentrer sur l'arbre exhibé – un arbre stylisé suivant une esthétique artificielle. La vraie nature est probablement trop forte, trop accablante pour être comprise; elle doit être simplifiée, rendue de plus en plus abstraite. Lorsque je compris ceci, je commençais à réaliser que l'abstraction et cer-

DER SUCHE NACH EINEM ANDEREN STIL

Als ich anfing Bonsai zu studieren, unterrichteten meine Lehrer mich nicht nur im Gießen, Schneiden und Drahten, sondern auch, daß Bonsai eine selbständige Kunstform ist. Ich lernte, daß ein Baum Stimmungen ausdrücken kann, die man mit menschlichen Emotionen vergleichen kann. Obwohl ein Baum wie ein Stein für einen Bildhauer ist, sollte er seine Stimmungen und Emotionen ausdrücken ohne dabei das Konzept Bonsai zu verlieren.

Als ich gelernt hatte, die Bonsaitechniken zu meistern, konnte ich die klassischen Stilarten von Bonsai gestalten, aber das befriedigte mich nicht. Natürlich kann sich jeder weiterentwickeln, ich jedoch suchte nach eine persönlichen Annäherung. Über Fragen wie 'Was macht Bonsai zur Kunst?' 'Ist Bonsai Kunst?' und 'Wo sind die Grenzen bei Bonsai als Kunst?' erbrach ich mir den Kopf. Auf diese Weise begann mein langer Pfad zwischen der Entwicklung meines eigene Stils und der Suche nach neuen Inspirationsquellen.

Im Gebirge werde ich durch die Art und Weise inspiriert, in der die Natur die Bäume formt. In Holland gibt es jedoch keine Natur in der Nahe - die holländische Landschaft ist sehr rational und funktionell. Ich habe bemerkt, daß diese in Japan, bis auf die Gebirge, ähnlich ist. Es gibt wenig Platz und der direkte Kontakt mit der freien Natur ist nicht möglich. So scheint es nur logisch zu sein, die Natur auf Bonsaiart zu verkleinern. Es erinnert an die wirkliche Natur in Stilisierter Form. Nur dann wenn Bonsai von der Natur isoliert ist, erreicht es seine höchste künstlerische Bedeutung. Die Tokonoma ist so ein idealer Platz. In der Tokonoma werden Bonsai von fremden Ablenkungen abgeschirmt so daß man sich auf den ausgestellten Baum konzentrieren kann - einen Baum, der nach Aspekten von menschlicher Ästhetik geformt wurde. Die pure Natur ist wahrscheinlich zu stark und zu überwältigend, um verstanden zu werden und muß vereinfacht werden. Wobei sie mehr und mehr abstrakt wird. Dieser Tatsache bewußt, begann ich zu erfassen, daß die Kombination

'The Whirlpool' Juniperus chinensis. Rock: Bryan Albright

'The Wreckage Juniperus chinensis. Rock: Bryan Albright

sculptor. Compared to bonsai, it is far more artistic and creative. In bonsai the focus is on the tree, whereas in ikebana the focus is on the whole composition which can consist of many different elements. The famous classical bonsai are examples of how modern Japanese masters translate the image of natural trees into more abstract, stylised forms. Understanding this made it clear to me how the Japanese evolved bonsai into the refined styles that exist today.

According to Zen, everything already exists in nature, hidden away for man to discover. We do not invent things out of the blue – everything evolves from something that was there before. We borrow ideas from our surroundings and give them our own interpretation.

Putting all these ideas and information together, I started making compositions which incorporated dead wood, rusted iron and differently designed pots which, when combined with the tree, give a very dramatic image. Just being original or creating different effects is not the goal in itself. I try hard to evoke certain moods, ranging from loneliness or melancholy to strength and stubbornness.

On these and the following pages you can see how my work changed as a result of this quest. This doesn't mean that I turned my back on classical bonsai, which is a valuable source of inspiration, but I consider it a noble craft rather than art. The Japanese style is the base from which I depart, trying to create more artistic and free works. This is a path with no rules and many risks – but isn't that what art is all about?

vitale, ha un'approccio molto aperto per quanto riguardo lo stile. In questo caso l'artista lavora con fiori, rami, pezzi di legno ecc, come un vero e proprio scultore, un'arte che a confronto del bonsai, è molto più artistica e creativa. Nel bonsai il punto focale e sull'albero, mentre nell'ikebana il punto focale è sull'intera composizione che può comprendere molti elementi. I famosi bonsai classici sono esempi di come i maestri giapponesi moderni traducono l'immagine di alberi in natura nelle forme più astratte e stilizzate. Comprendendo tutto questo mi fu chiaro come i giapponesi hanno evoluti il bonsai negli stili raffinati che esistono oggi.

Secondo lo Zen ogni cosa esiste già nella natura ma è nascosta aspettando solo che l'uomo la scopra. Non inventiamo cose per caso, ogni cosa evolve da ciò che ci fu nascosto prima. Noi prendiamo le idee dall'ambiente e li interpretiamo come vogliamo.

Mettendo assieme queste idee ed informazioni iniziai a creare composizioni incorporando legno morto, ferro arrugginito e vasi di diverse forme che, una volta unite con gli alberi, creavano un'immagine molto drammatica. Lo scopo di questa ricerca non era trovare forzatamente l'originalità e la diversità. Ho cercato di trasmettere con le piante diversi sentimenti e sensazioni come la solitudine o la malinconia, la forza e testardaggine.

Su queste pagine e quelle che seguono si può notare l'evoluzione del mio lavoro che è sempre corso parallelamente alla mia ricerca personale. Ciò non vuol dire che ho girato le spalle al bonsai classico, il quale rimarrà sempre una grande fonte d'ispirazione, ma lo considero un'abilità nobile piuttosto che un'arte. Lo stile giapponese rappresenta per me la partenza di un viaggio che mi porterà a creare lavori più artistici e liberi. Questa è la strada senza regole e con molti rischi – ma non è proprio questo il senso d'arte?

mentos clave en este arte.

La ikebana moderna, donde la abstracción es tambien vital, tiene una manera muy abierta de estilización. Aquí el artista trabaja con flores, ramajes, pedazos de madera, como un escultor. En comparación con el bonsai es mucho más artístico y creativo. En bonsai el foco principal está en el árbol mismo mientras que en ikebana el foco reside en el conjunto de la composición formada de diversos elementos. El famoso bonsai clásico es el ejemplo de cómo los grandes maestros modernos japoneses interpretan la imagen de los arboles naturales en algo de formas más abstractas y estilizadas. Comprendido esto, está claro cómo los japoneses han evolucionado el bonsai hasta poder obtener los estilos refinados que existen hoy.

Según Zen, todo existe ya en la naturaleza, escondido alrededor para ser descubierto. Nadie inventa algo de la nada – todo evoluciona de algo que ya existía previamente. Tomamos ideas prestadas de nuestros alrededores, y las devolvemos con nuestra propia interpretación.

Recopilando todas estas ideas e informaciones juntas, comencé a crear composiciones incorporando madera seca, hierro oxidado y diferentes macetas de diseño las cuales al ser combinadas con el árbol daban una imagen muy dramática. Ser simplemente original o crear efectos diferentes no es la meta en sí. Trato más bién de evocar diferentes sentimientos, que alternan desde tristeza o melancolía hasta fuerza y terquedad.

En estas primeras páginas y las siguientes podréis ver cuanto ha cambiado mi trabajo como resultado de esta búsqueda. Esto no quiere decir que halla dado la espalda al bonsai clásico, el cual es una valiosa fuente de inspiración, pero si lo considero más una destreza que un arte. El estilo japonés es la base fundamental, la cual utilizo como punto de partida para crear una forma más artística y libre. Es este un camino sin reglas y con muchos riesgos – pero, ¿no es eso de lo que se trata el arte?

tains principes esthétiques forment les éléments clés de cette forme d'art.

L'ikebana moderne, ou l'abstraction est aussi vitale, permet une approche très libre envers la création d'une forme. L'artiste travaille avec des fleurs, des branches, des morceaux de bois etc, comme un sculpteur. Comparé au bonsaï, c'est beaucoup plus artistique et créatif. En bonsaï, le centre d'intérêt est l'arbre, alors qu'en ikebana, c'est toute la composition, qui est d'ailleurs souvent composée de plusieurs éléments differents. Les bonsaïs classiques les plus appréciés démontrent que les maîtres Japonais modernes développent des formes stylisées et abstraites pour représenter les arbres sauvages. Lorsque je compris ceci, je compris comment les Japonais développèrent les bonsaïs de style raffiné qui existent de nos jours.

D'après le zen, tout existe déjà dans la nature, caché, attendant d'être découvert. Nous ne créons rien, tout évolue à partir d'une chose qui existait déjà. Nous empruntons des idées autour de nous et leur donnons notre interprétation personnelle.

J'ai réuni toutes ces idées, toutes ces informations et j'ai commencé à composer des scènes avec du bois mort, du fer rouillé, des coupes à bonsaï de styles différents, qui, avec l'arbre, produisent un effet dramatique. Le but en lui-même n'est pas simplement l'originalité ou la création d'effets nouveaux. J'essaye d'évoquer des humeurs allant de la solitude ou la mélancolie à la force et l'obstination.

Sur ces pages et les suivantes, vous verrez comment mon travail a evolué grâce à cette approche. Ceci ne veut pas dire que je rejette l'art bonsaï classique; il reste pour moi une source d'inspiration, mais je le perçois plutôt comme un type d'artisanat qu'un art. Le style Japonais m'a offert une base dont je m'éloigne maintenant, en essayant de créer une oeuvre plus libre et artistique. C'est un chemin sans règle et plein de risques – mais n'est-ce pas la nature même de l'art?

aus Abstraktion und Ästhetik Schlüsselelemente dieser Kunstform sind.

Moderne Ikebana, bei der die Abstraktion auch wesentlich ist, hat eine sehr offene Einstellung zur Gestaltungsweise. Hier arbeitet der Künstler wie ein echter Bildhauer, nur daß er Blumen, Zweige Holzstücke usw. benutzt. Verglichen mit Bonsai ist Ikebana viel künstlerischer und kreativer. Bei Bonsai liegt der Focus auf dem Baum, während bei Ikebana der Focus auf der Gesamtkomposition, die aus vielen verschiedenen Elementen bestehen kann, liegt. Die berühmten, klassischen Bonsai sind Beispiele da für, wie moderne japanische Meister das Bild eines Baumes in der Natur in abstraktere, stilisierte Formen interpretieren. Als ich dies verstanden hatte, wurde mir klar, wie die Japaner Bonsai in die verfeinerten Stilarten entwickelten wie3 sie heutzutage existieren.

Gemäß Zen existiert alles bereits in der Natur, nur für Menschen versteckt. Wir erfinden Sachen nicht aus dem *Nichts* heraus - alles entwickelt sich aus etwas, das bereits vorher existierte. Von unserer Umgebung entleihen wir Ideen und geben ihnen unsere eigene Deutung. Nachdem ich all diese Ideen und Informationen gesammelt hatte, begann ich Kompositionen zu machen, denen ich totes Holz, rostiges Eisen und verschieden gestaltete Schalen einverleibte. Zusammen mit dem Baum erzeugte das einen sehr dramatischen Eindruck. Aber das Ziel ist nicht originell zu sein oder verschiedene Effekte zu schaffen. Ich versuche sehr verschiedene Stimmungen hervorzurufen, und zwar von Einsamkeit oder Melancholie bis hin zur stärke und Sturheit. Auf dieser und auf den nächsten Seiten können Sie sehen, wie sich meine Arbeit als Resultat diese Nachforschens veränderte. Das heißt jedoch nicht, daß ich den klassischen Bonsai den Rücken zu kehre. Sie sind eine wertvolle Quelle der Inspiration, aber ich halte sie mehr für Kunst. Der japanische Stil ist die Basis von der ich ausgehe bei dem versuch künstlerischere und freiere Arbeiten zu schaffen. Diese ist ein Pfad ohne Regeln, jedoch mit vielen Risiken - aberist das nicht genau das, was Kunst ausmacht?

Juniperus chinensis
Rock: Bryan Albright

'The Burned Out' Juniperus chinensis.
Rock: William van Vlaanderen

Pinus Thunberghii
↕ 80cm
± 70 years / jahre / anni / ans / años
Japan
Tokoname

Cupressus

⇕ 60cm

70 years / jahre / anni / ans / años

Italy

Jon Dawson

◀ *'Flying Dutchman'*
Pinus parviflora
⬍ 65cm
23 years / jahre / anni / ans / años
Japan
⬓ Jassu Kaneko

▲ **Pinus parviflora**
⬍ 45cm
23 years / jahre / anni / ans / años
Japan
⬓ Farrand Bloch

Patrizio Fermani

Patrizio Fermani's passion for bonsai started around the mid-seventies. At the beginning of the eighties he started playing an active part in the Italian bonsai scene, taking part with his bonsai in the very first bonsai exhibitions. As secretary of AIB (Associazione Italiana Bonsai) since 1992 until it was dissolved in 1995, he was one of the most convinced supporters of re-uniting Italian bonsai. He was a founder member of UBI (Unione Bonsaisti Italiani) and is currently director acting as secretary. Apart from participating in the major collective exhibitions of Italian and foreign bonsai, obtaining numerous prizes and mentions, 1977 UBI prize being one of them, his bonsai have been exhibited at many personal shows throughout Italy. He has written many articles for Italian and foreign bonsai magazines. His personal collection comprises around 100 bonsai. He travels often to Japan to study bonsai, from the First World Bonsai Congress in Omiya in 1989, to the most important shows; Kokufu-ten in Tokyo, Taikan-ten in Kyoto, etc. He has visited the most important gardens and collections of bonsai in Japan, and is a pupil of Kunio Kobayashi who is one of the principal Japanese bonsai experts. Occasionally he travels to the showroom of the master in Tokyo where he lives and works throughout his stay in Japan.

Inizia ad interessarsi di bonsai intorno alla metà degli anni settanta. All'inizio degli anni ottanta incomincia a muoversi attivamente nel panorama del bonsaismo italiano, partecipando con i suoi bonsai alle prime mostre italiane. Segretario dell'AIB (Associazione Italiana Bonsai) dal 1992 al 1995 anno del suo scioglimento, è stato uno dei più convinti sostenitori della riunificazione del bonsai italiano. Socio Fondatore dell'UBI (Unione Bonsaisti Italiani) ne è attualmente Consigliere con incarico di Segretario. Oltre a partecipare alle principali esposizioni collettive di bonsai italiane e straniere, ottenendo numerosi premi e riconoscimenti, tra i quali il Premio UBI 1997, i suoi bonsai sono stati esposti in decine di mostre personali in tutta Italia. Ha scritto innumerevoli articoli per le riviste italiane è straniere di bonsai. la sua collezione personale è attualmente costituita da circa 100 bonsai. Frequenti sono i suoi viaggi i Giappone per studiare il bonsai; dal 1º Congresso Mondiale del Bonsai di Omiya nel 1989, alle principali mostre, kokufu-ten di Tokyo, Taikan-ten di Kyoto ecc. Ha visitato i più importanti giardini e collezioni bonsai del Giappone. Allievo di Kunio Kobayaschi, uno dei maggiori esponenti del bonsai Giapponese, periodicamente si reca nell'atelier del maestro in Tokyo dove vive e lavora per il periodo della sua permanenza in Giappone.

◀ **Cupressus sempervirens**

⇕ 51cm   ◁▷ 55cm

Seed / sämling / semina / graine / semilla

Tokoname

La pasión de Patrizio Fermani por bonsai surgió sobre la mitad de los setenta. A comienzos de los ochenta empezó a tomar parte de la escena de bonsai italiana, participando con su bonsai en las primeras exhibiciones de entonces. Como secretario de AIB (Associazione Italiana Bonsai) desde 1992 hasta su disolución en 1995, él era uno de los partidiarios más convincentes para la reconciliación del Bonsai italiano. Fué uno de los miembros fundadores de UBI (Unione Bonsaisti Italiani) y en la actualidad está desempeñando el cargo de secretario. Aparte de participar en importantes exhibiciones colectivas de bonsai italiano además de extranjeras, y obtener numerosos premios y menciones, (el premio UBI 1977 entre ellos) su bonsai ha estado exhibido en muchas demostraciones propias a través de Italia. Ha escrito, por otra parte un gran número de artículos para revistas de bonsai italianas además de extranjeras. Su colección privada comprende aproximadamente 100 bonsais. Patrizio viaja frecuentemente a Japón para estudiar bonsai, desde en el "First World Bonsai Congres" en Omiya en 1989 hasta el show más importante; Kokufu-Ten en Tokyo o Taikan-Ten, en Kyoto, etc. Ha visitado los jardines y colecciones de bonsai japoneses más importantes, y es alumno de Kunio Kobayaschi, uno de los expertos de bonsai japoneses más destacados. En ocasiones viaja al taller del maestro japonés en Tokyo donde Patrizio se aloja y trabaja durante su estancia en Japón.

La passion de Patrizio Fermani pour les bonsaïs a commencé dans les années soixante dix. Au début des années quatre vingts, Patrizio commence à jouer un rôle actif dans le milieu des bonsaïs Italiens, et à prendre part aux toutes premières expositions avec des bonsaïs. En tant que secrétaire de l'AIB (Associazione Italiana Bonsai) depuis 1992, jusqu'à sa dissolution en 1995, il croyait fermement à la réunification du bonsaï Italien. Il est un des membres fondateurs de l'UBI (Unione Bonsaisti Italiani) dont il est directeur et secrétaire. Il participe à toutes les expositions principales de bonsaïs Italiens et étrangers et gagne de nombreuses mentions et prix, l'un d'entre eux le prix UBI 1997. Ses bonsaïs sont aussi exhibés dans beaucoup d'expositions personnelles à travers toute l'Italie. Il a écrit beaucoup d'articles pour des magazines Italiens et étrangers. Il a plus de 100 arbres dans sa collection personnelle. Il va régulièrement au Japon pour étudier les bonsaïs, depuis le Premier Congrès Mondial du Bonsaï à Omiya en 1989, aux spectacles les plus importants; Kokufu-ten à Tokyo, Taikan-ten à Kyoto, etc. Il a visité les jardins et les collections les plus importants du Japon et est l'élève de Kunio Kobayaschi, l'un des principaux experts en bonsaï au Japon. De temps en temps, il se rend à l'atelier du maître à Tokyo où il vit et travaille durant son séjour au Japon.

Seine Leidenschaft für Bonsai begann Mitte der siebziger Jahre. Anfang der achtziger Jahre spielte er schon eine aktive Rolle in der italienischen Bonsaiszene, in dem er mit seinen Bonsai an den ersten Ausstellunger teilnahm. Als Geschäftsführer der AIB (Associanzone Italiana Bonsai) von 1992 an bis 1995 (in diesem Jahre wurde der Verband aufgelöst) war er einer der gröflten Verfechter für die Wiedervereinigung italienischer Bonsaiverbände. Er war Gründungsmitglied der VBI (Unione Bonsaisiti Italiani) und ist einer der Direktion und fungiert als Geschäftsführer.

Seine Bonsai haben bei groflen Gemeinschaftsausstellungen italienischer und ausländischer Bonsai zahlreiche Preise und Urkunden gewonnen, darunter der Preis der UBI 1997. Seine Bonsai wurden auch auf persönlichen Ausstellungen in ganz Italien ausgestellt. Er hat für italienische und ausländische Bonsaimagazine viele Artikel geschrieben. Seine persönliche Sammlung besteht aus ca. 100 Bonsai.

Patrizio reist oft nach Japan um Bonsai zu studieren, vom 1. Kongrefl der WBFF in Omiya im Jahr 1089, zu den bedeutendsten Ausstellungen, wie z.B. der Kokufu-Ten in Tokyo, der Taikan-Ten in Kyoto usw. Er hat in Japan die wichtigsten Gärten und Sammlungen besucht. Er ist Schüler von Kunio Kobayaschi, der einer der gröflten Experten Japans ist. Von Zeit zu Zeit reist er zum Ausstellungsraum seines Meisters in Tokyo, bei dem er während seiner Aufenthalte lebt und arbeitet.

FERMANI
ARCHITETTURA DEL PAESAGGIO

Patrizio Fermani
Studio Fermani, Via G Brodolini 14,
63020 Montappone (AP), Italy
Tel: +39 (0)734-760575
Fax: +39 (0)734-761022

Patrizio Fermani

RAFT OF JUNIPERUS COMMUNIS

Of the many bonsai styles surely the one that deserves particular attention is the raft. Bonsai styled in this way are in fact rarely exhibited. It is true that to create a good quality bonsai takes a long time but sometimes you can 'manage' to find the right material which, with a lot of expertise but a little time and work, can have exceptional results. This is not applicable to the raft style because the part from the roots to the foliage has to be built with care and patience. The starting material should be chosen with care and trees should be selected for their crawling appearance and with branches that only grow on one side. The term raft indicates a fallen tree, whose trunk is buried and the branches grow, slowly but surely, vertically like trunks.

The main difference between the 'multiple trunk' and 'raft' style is the following: the first are made from trees which are planted singularly and taught to grow together, the second is characterised by a single tree the branches of which are taught to become individual trees, therefore it is important that the position of each single branch along the trunk should be taken into account. Most of the plants generally used for bonsai can be utilised for the raft style; great importance should be given however to the predisposition of the species to produce roots from the trunk and branches. Of all species, one that is particularly interesting for the results which can be obtained as bonsai is the common juniper (Juniperus Communis). The photos which accompany this article show the various phases in the formation of a juniper in the raft style.

Photo 1 (April 1984) the plant was collected in the mountains at a height of around 1400 metres; it comes from a bush of about 1.6m diameter. The trunk was growing against the ground and the branches also had the same characteristic. This creeping appearance was due to the strong wind, which prevented arboreal growth, and the snow which is present

ZATTERA DI JUNIPERUS COMMUNIS

Tra i tanti stili bonsai sicuramente merita un'attenzione particolare lo stile a zattera, infatti raramente si vedono esposti esemplari in questo affascinante stile. E' vero che per creare un bonsai di buona qualità occorrono tempi lunghi, ma a volte, capita di trovare del "materiale" molto valido che con molta perizia , ma con poco tempo e lavoro più portare ad ottenere degli ottimi risultati. Per lo stile a zattera questo non è possibile in quanto, dall'apparato radicale alla chioma, tutto deve essere costruito con cura e pazienza. Il materiale di partenza deve essere selezionato con cura, preferibilmente vanno scelte piante con portamento strisciante e con rami che crescono da un solo lato. Il termine zattera indica un albero caduto il cui tronco si interra ed i rami crescono, a poco a poco, verticalmente come tronchi. La principale differenza fra lo "Stile a zattera" e lo "Stile tronchi multipli" è la seguente: il primo è costituito da alberi piantati singolarmente ed educati a crescere insieme, il secondo è caratterizzato da un solo albero i cui rami sono educati per diventare alberi individuali, quindi necessariamente bisogna tenere conto della posizione che ogni singolo ramo occupa lungo il tronco. La maggior parte delle piante comunemente usati per bonsai, possono essere utilizzati per lo stile a zattera; grande importanza deve comunque essere data alla predisposizione dell'albero ad emettere radici dal tronco e dai rami. Fra le specie , una particolarmente interessante, per i risultati che si ottengono come bonsai, è il ginepro communis (Juniperus Communis). Le foto che accompagnano l'articolo illustrano le varie fasi occorse per la formazione di un ginepro nello stile a zattera.

Foto 1 (aprile 1984), la pianta è stata raccolta in montagna a circa 1400 mt di altitudine; si presenta come un cespuglio di 1.60 circa di diametro. Il tronco si sviluppa aderente al terreno ed anche i rami si presentano con la stessa caratteristica. Questo portamento strisciante è dovu-

BALSA DEL JUNIPERUS COMMUNIS

De los muchos estilos de bonsai, seguramente uno de los que merece atención especial es el "balsa".

El bonsai estilizado de esta forma es de hecho muy raramente exhibido. Es verdad que el crear un bonsai de calidad consume mucho tiempo, pero a veces uno "se las arregla" para encontrar el material idóneo, el cual con la debida experiencia y un poquito de tiempo y trabajo, puede dar un resultado final excepcional. Este ejemplo no se puede aplicar al estilo balsa debido a que desde la raíz hasta la fronda debe de ser "construido" con cuidado y paciencia. El material primordial debe de ser elejido meticulosamente y los arboles deben de ser seleccionados por su apariencia trepadora y con ramas que brotan solamente por un lado del tronco. El termino balsa indica un "árbol caido", cuyo tronco esta enterrado y las ramas crecen, lentas pero seguras, y verticalmente como los troncos mismos.

Las diferencias más notables entre el "tronco múltiple" y el estilo "balsa" son los siguientes: el primero consiste en arboles que están plantados de una manera singular y dispuestos a crecer juntos, el segundo se caracteriza por un solo árbol cuyas ramas están predispuestas para crecer como árboles individuales.

Por lo tanto es importante que la posición de cada rama a través del tronco sea tomada en consideración. La gran mayoria de plantas que se usan para bonsai pueden adoptarse para el estilo "balsa"; aunque si se debe dar gran importancia a la predisposición de la planta para producir raices del tronco y ramas. De todas las especies, una que es particularmente interesante por los resultados que podemos obtener como bonsai es el junípero común (Juniperus Comunis). Las fotografías que acompañan este artículo nos demuestran las diferentes fases en la formación de un junipero en el estilo "balsa".

Fotografía I (Abril 1984) La planta fué recogida en las montañas a una altura de aproximadamente 1400 metros; procede de un arbusto de 1,6 metros de diámetro. El

RADEAU DE JUNIPERUS COMMUNIS

L'un des nombreux styles de bonsaï qui mérite le plus d'attention est le radeau. Les bonsaïs stylisés en forme de radeau sont dailleurs rarement exposés. Il est vrai que créer un bonsaï de qualité prend longtemps mais il est parfois possible de trouver la matière première idéale, qui, avec beaucoup de savoir faire mais peu de temps et de travail, peut produire des résultats exceptionnels. Ceci ne s'applique pas au style du radeau parceque la section des racines au feuillage doit être construite avec attention et patience. Le matériel de base doit être choisi avec attention: les arbres sélectionnés pour leur apparence rampante, et leurs branches ne poussant que d'un coté. Le terme «radeau» décrit un arbre abattu, dont le tronc est enseveli, dont les branches poussent, lentement mais sûrement, verticalement, comme des troncs.

La différence principale entre le style «tronc multiple» et le style «radeau» est la suivante: le premier est composé d'arbres qui sont plantés individuellement et que l'on entraîne à pousser en groupe, le second est caracterisé par un seul arbre dont les branches sont formées comme des arbres individuels, il est donc important de prendre en compte la position de chaque branche le long du tronc. La plupart des plantes utilisées pour les bonsaïs peuvent être adaptées au style radeau; la prédisposition de l'espèce à produire des racines venant du tronc et des branches est de la plus grande importance. De toutes les espèces, l'une d'elles est trés intéressante pour les résultats qu'elle produit: le genévrier commun (Juniperus communis). Les photos qui accompagnent cet article montrent les différentes étapes de la formation d'un genévrier en style radeau.

Photo 1 (avril 1984) la plante a été recueillie dans les montagnes à une altitude de 1400 mètres. Elle vient d'un buisson d'environ 1,6 mètre de diamètre. Le tronc poussait sur le sol et les branches avaient la même caractéristique. Cette

FLOßFORM EINES JUNIPERUS COMMUNIS

Von den vielen Bonsaistilarten verdient eine Stilart besondere Beachtung - die Floflform. Bonsai in dieser Stilart werden tatsächlich nur selten ausgestellt. Es stimmt, dafl es sehr lange dauert bis man einen Bonsai von guter Qualität gestalten kann. Aber manchmal hat man 'Glück' und findet Material, welches man mit groflem Sachverstand, aber mit wenig Zeit - und Arbeitsaufwand, außerordentliche Resultate erzielt.

Bei der Floßform ist das leider nicht möglich, denn von den Wurzeln bis zu den Blättern muß alles sorgfältig und geduldig aufgebaut werden. Das Ausgangsmaterial muß sorgfältig ausgesucht werden. Die Bäume sollten ein 'kriechendes' Aussehen haben und Äste, die nur auf einer Seite wachsen. 'Floßform' bezeichnet einen umgestürzten Baum dessen Stamm begraben ist und dessen Äste langsam aber stetig, wie Stämme nach oben wachsen.

Der Hauptunterschied zwischen der Floßform und einem Mehrfachstamm ist folgender: Mehrfachstamm wird aus einzelnen Bäumen gestaltet, die einzeln gepflanzt werden und dazu erzogen werden, zusammenzuwachsen, die Floßform wird durch einen Baum charakterisiert, dessen Äste dazu erzogen werden, individuelle Bäume zu werden. Darum ist es wichtig, daß man die Position jedes einzelnen Astes am Stamm berücksichtigt. Die meisten Pflanzen, die man allgemein für Bonsai gebrauchen kann, eignen sich auch für die Floßform. Sehr wichtig ist es jedoch, daß die Planze dazu neigt am Stamm und an den Ästen Wurzeln zu bilden.

Für die Floßform bei Bonsai ist eine Art besonders geeignet und zwar der 'Gemeine Wacholder' (Juniperus communis). Die Fotos, die diesen Bericht begleiten, zeigen die verschiedenen Phasen der Gestaltung eines Wacholders zu Floßform.

Foto 1 (April 1984): Deie Pflanze wurde in den Bergen in einer Höhe von 1400 Metern gesammelt. Die Pflanze war ein Busch mit einem Durchmesser von 160 Zentimetern. Der Stamm wächst zur Erde hin und auch die Äste zeigen diese Tendenz. Das

2

3

most months of the year.

Photo 2 (August 1984) the plant after being collected is re-potted in a large container. The trunk is positioned horizontally while the branches have been straightened using wire.

Photo 3 (June 1988) Only after the plant has had a resting period and produced abundant growth can it be re-potted in a specially prepared large wooden box. The trunk is planted in a horizontal position including the branches (drawing 1). The wire which is tied tightly to the bark, apart from keeping the branches in place also serves to stimulate the growth of roots in that point. In fact as the branch grows the wire will interrupt the natural circulation of the descending sap, favouring the growth of new roots. In September 1989 the plant was removed from the wooden trough and put into the definitive bonsai pot. The numerous capillary roots which had grown in the meantime enabled the soil to be reduced enough to allow me to re-pot the bonsai in a pot only a few centimetres high.

Photo 4 (May 1990) the plant has been allowed to grow freely and both the trunk and the branches have grown notably stronger. The following pruning, wiring and pinching have allowed the foliage of each trunk to be integrated, giving them a more natural and realistic aspect.

to al forte vento, che impedisce una vegetazione arborea, ed allo schiacciamento da parte della neve presente per molti mesi all'anno.

Foto 2 (Agosto 1984), la pianta, dopo la raccolta, viene invasata in un capiente contenitore. il tronco si presenta orizzontalmente, mentre i rami sono stati raddrizzati con l'ausilio del filo metallico.

Foto 3 (Giugno 1988), solo dopo un'abbondante risposta vegetativa viene effettuato il primo rinvaso in una capiente cassa di legno appositamente preparata. Il tronco viene interrato in posizione orizzontale compresa la base dei rami (dis.1) .Il filo metallico, legato ben stretto sulla corteccia, oltre a tenere in posizione i vari rami, serve anche a stimolare l'emissione di radici in quel punto, infatti con la crescita del ramo, il filo creerà una interruzione alla naturale circolazione della linfa discendente favorendo così la creazione di nuove radici. Nel settembre 1989, la pianta è stata estratta dalla cassa di legno e sistemata nel definitivo vaso bonsai; le numerose radici capillari formatesi nel frattempo hanno consentito una notevole riduzione del pane di terra da permettere il rinvaso in un contenitore bonsai di pochi centimetri d'altezza.

Foto 4 (Maggio 1990) la pianta è stata lasciata vegetare liberamente, così facendo si è avuto un notevole irrobustimento dei tronchi e dei rami. I successivi interventi di potatura, legatura e pizzicatura hanno consentito l'integrazione delle chiome dei vari tronchi, conferendogli un aspetto sempre più naturale e realistico.

tronco estaba creciendo a ras del suelo y las ramas también cumplen estas características. Esta apariencia trepadora, se debe a los fuertes vientos que desfavorecen el crecimiento arbóreo, además de la nieve, que aquí esta presente la mayor parte del año.

Fotografia 2 (Agosto 1984) La planta después de haber sido recogida es trasplantada a una maceta más amplia. El tronco está colocado horizontalmente mientras que las ramas se enderezan mediante el uso de alambres.

Fotografia 3 (Junio 1988) Unicamente después de haberle permitido a la planta un periodo de descanso y que haya adquirido un crecimiento abundante, puede ser trasplantada en una caja de madera especialmente preparada. El tronco es plantado en posición horizontal incluyendo las ramas (dibujo n.1). El alambre con el que se le aprieta fuertemente a la corteza, aparte de mantener las ramas en posición, desempeña un papel importante estimulando el crecimiento de las raices en ese punto. De hecho a la vez que la rama crece el alambre interrumpe la circulación natural en el descenso de la savia, favoreciendo el brote de raices nuevas. En septiembre de 1989 la planta fué nuevamente trasplantada de la caja de madera a su tiesto definitivo. Las numerosas raices capilares, que crecieron durante este tiempo habian reducido el espacio de suelo lo suficiente para poder trasplantar el bonsai a una maceta de apenas unos centimetros de altura.

Fotografia 4 (Mayo 1990) Una vez permitido el crecimiento libre, ambos tronco y ramas han desarrollado notablemente más fuertes. La poda,el alambrado y el pinzado posteriores han permitido la integración del follaje en cada tronco, dando a estos últimos un aspecto más natural y reaistico.

apparence rampante est dûe au vent puissant qui empêche la pousse et à la neige présente presque toute l'année.

Photo 2 (août 1984) la plante après avoir été recueillie est rempotée dans un grand bac. Le tronc est posé horizontalement et les branches sont rendues plus droites par des fils d'aluminium.

Photo 3 (juin 1988) après un repos et la production d'une pousse abondante, la plante peut être rempotée dans une grande boite de bois faite exprès. Le tronc est planté dans la position horizontale et les branches sont tenues droites par des fils d'aluminium attachés au fond de la bate (dessin 1). Les fils d'aluminium qui sont attachés serrés à l'écorce, tiennent les branches en place mais servent aussi à stimuler la croissance des racines en ces endroits. Quand la branche grossit, les fils interrompent la circulation de la sève dans sa descente, ce qui encourage la pousse de nouvelles racines. En septembre 1989, la plante fut retirée de sa boite de bois et plantée dans son pot definitif. Les nombreuses racines secondaires qui ont poussé entre temps permettent la reduction de la quantité de sol nécessaire. Je peux donc rempoter le bonsaï dans un pot de quelques centimètres de profondeur.

Photo 4 (mai 1990) on a laissé la plante pousser librement et le tronc et les branches sont beaucoup plus vigoureux. L'élagage, le ligaturage et le pincement qui suivirent ont permis à chaque tronc d'être integré, ce qui leur donne un aspect plus naturel et réaliste.

Key to illustration
1wooden trough; 2 bottom slats; 3 feet; 4 drainage net; 5 nails to anchor the guys; 6 rope handles; 7 original root ball; 8 aluminium wire guys; 9 tying, the exact point should be carefully evaluated as the roots will grow there.

Legenda desegno
1 cassa di legno; 2 doghe di fondo; 3 piedini; 4 retina di drenaggio; 5 chiodi per ancoraggio tiranti; 6 manici di corda; 7 zolla originale; 8 tiranti in filo di alluminio; 9 legatura, il punto esatto deve essere valutato attentamente in quanto è qui che si formeranno le nuove radici.

Referencias
1 Caja de madera; 2 Tablillas de fondo; 3 Pies; 4 Red de desagüe; 5 Puntas para el anclaje de los tensores; 6 Asas de la cuerda; 7 Esfera de la raiz original; 8 Tensores de alambre de aluminio; 9 Al tensar, el punto exacto debe de ser cuidadosamente valorado ya que precisamente ahí mismo brotarán las raices.

Légende des dessins
1 bac de bois; 2 lattes du fond; 3 pieds; 4 filet d'evacuation; 5 clous pour ancrer les fils d'aluminium; 6 poignées; 7 boule des racines du depart; 8 fils d'aluminium; 9 attachement.

kriechende Aussehen rührt von starken Winden her, die eine Baum Vegetation verhindern. Auch der Schnee, der die meiste Zeit des Jahres da ist, trägt dazu bei.

Foto 2 (Aug. 1984) Die Pflanze wurde nach dem Sammeln in ein großes Gefäß umgepflanzt. Der Stamm wurde horizontal positioniert, während die Äste mit Hilfe von Draht ausgerichtet wurden.

Foto 3 (Juni 1988) Nur wenn die Pflanze eine ausreichende Vegetationsperiode zum Erholen hatte, kann sie in eine spezielle vorbereitete, große Holzkiste umgetopft werden. Der Stamm wird mit den Ästen in eine horizontale Position gepflanzt (Zeichnung 1). Der Metalldraht, der eng um den Stamm gedrahtet wird, hält nicht nur die Äste an ihrem Platz sondern dient auch dazu, das Wurzelwachstum an dieser Stelle zu stimulieren. Wenn der Ast nämlich wächst, unterbricht der Draht den natürlichen Kreislauf der herabsteigenden Lymphbahnen, und begünstigt so das neue Wurzelwachstum. Im September 1989 wurde die Pflanze aus der Holzkiste herausgenommen und in die endgültige Bonsaischale gesetzt. Die zahlreichen Kapillarwurzeln, die in der Zwischenzeit gewachsen waren, hatten die Erde genug reduziert, daß man den Bonsai in eine Schale pflanzen konnte, die nur wenige Zentimeter hoch ist.

Foto 4 (Mai 1990) Die fplanze durfte sich frei entwickeln und der Stamm und die Äste sind bemerkenswert stärker geworden. Durch Schneiden, Drahten und Pinzieren hat sich das Laub jedes Stammes so integriert, daß es einen natürlicheren und realisterischen Anblick hat.

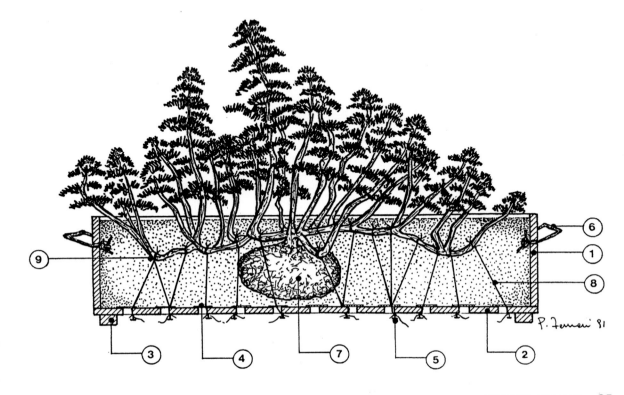

Die Aufschlüsselung der Zeichnung:
1 Holztrog; 2 Bodenleiste; 3 Füße;
4 Abzugsnetze; 5 Nägel zum Verankern der Taue; 6 Seilgriffe; 7 Originalerde; 8 Taue aus Aluminiumdraht; 9 Verankerung, der genaue Punkt sollte sorgfältig bestimmt werden, da hier die Wurzeln wachsen.

PATRIZIO FERMANI **25**

◀ **Taxus baccata**
⬍ 43cm ◁▷ 52cm
Yamadori 1992
⏖ Korea

▶ **Ostrya carpinifolia**
⬍ 55cm ◁▷ 58cm
Yamadori 1987
⏖ Japan

ENGLAND

Colin Lewis

GB

Colin Lewis has been growing bonsai for 22 years, spending the first ten concentrating on shohin. "I had no idea how big a bonsai was supposed to be," he claims.

During this period Colin had become proficient in all the basic techniques such as repotting, pruning, wiring and, to an extent, the aesthetic side of bonsai. "I used to work on my bonsai every evening, plus most weekends. This constant practice means that the techniques become second nature so you're not preoccupied with them – you can concentrate on the design and planning for future development."

Colin Lewis was born in 1946 and was brought up in the lush green countryside of southern England, where trees were every boys' playground. Having been trained in graphic design, which he still practises professionally, it is inevitable that he has some pretty strong ideas about the bonsai image. "Nowadays, each bonsai I create must be different – as original as possible. I don't have much interest in slavishly following classic Japanese styles any more, although I still believe it is a good discipline to learn."

Colin believes that we should all draw upon our own artistic and cultural heritage to create ever-more imaginative and evocative images. "After all, there's no point in trying to evoke images of an entirely alien land and culture, is there?" But he admits to one source of inspiration that is common to all bonsai enthusiasts – that fanciful landscape of the mind, where anything is possible.

A former board member of the European Bonsai Association, Colin Lewis is currently consultant to Bonsai magazine in the UK, a judge at the Chelsea Flower Show and author of four books and countless magazine articles. He regularly teaches in his own studio and at major events throughout Europe and in the United States.

I

Colin Lewis coltiva bonsai da 22 anni, dieci dei quali dedicati agli shohin. Questo periodo ha dato a Colin una preparazione tecnica molto avanzata negli interventi come, rinvasi, potature, applicazione del filo.

'Lavoravo su i miei bonsai tutte le sere e la maggior parte dei fine settimana. Questo continuo esercizio mi ha reso padrone delle tecniche e questa sicurezza mi ha permesso di concentrarmi, approfondendo il disegno e la pianifacazione degli interventi futuri di tuute le mie piante'.

Colin Lewis è nato nel 1946, ed è cresciuto in mezzo al verde nel sud d'Inghilterra, dove gli alberi sono campi da gioco per ogni ragazzino. La sua visione del bonsai è stata favorita dalla preparazione artistica avendo seguito gli studi come grafico, pertanto Colin haidee sugli stili che sono certamente d'avanguardia. 'Ogni bonsai che oggi creo deve essere differente e più originale possibile. Non ho molto interesse a seguire gli stili giapponese, anche se credo che comunque vadano acquisiti come concetto di base'. Questo artista è convinto che per creare nuove forme più originali e al contempo più evocative si debba fare ricorso al proprio bagaglio artistico-culturale. 'Non ha alcun senso cercare di rappresentare paesi e cultura assulutamente astruse'.

Tuttavia ammette una sua fonte di ispirazione comune a tutti i bonsaisti: 'qyel bel paesaggio della mente, dove qualunque cosa è possibile'.

E' stato socio del consiglio Direttivo della European Bonsai Association, ed è attualmente consulente dela rivista Bonsai nel Regno Unito, giudice alla Chelsea Flower Show, ed autore di 4 libri ed innumerevoli articoli per riviste.

Regolarmente insegna nel suo studio ed ai maggiori congressi Europei e negli Stati Uniti.

▲ **Larix decidua**
⇕ 57cm   ◁▷ 58cm
17 years

Seed / sämling / semina /
graine / semilla

Colin Lewis ha estado cultivando bonsai durante 22 años, los primeros diez años concentrándose principalmente en "shohin". "No tenía la mínima idea del tamaño que debía de ser un bonsai" nos cuenta. Durante este periodo Colin ha llegado a ser competente en todas las técnicas básicas como el transplante, la poda, el alambrado y hasta cierto punto, de la parte estética de bonsai. "Yo solía trabajar en mi bonsai todas las tardes, además de casi todos los fines de semana. Esta práctica constante significa que las técnicas vienen a ser como una segunda naturaleza, por lo tanto no nos preocupamos tanto en ellas - podemos de esta manera concentrarnos en el diseño y la planificación para un futuro desarrollo."

Colin Lewis nació en 1946 y fué criado en el exhuberante verde de la campiña del sur de Inglaterra, donde los arboles eran el "recreo" de cualquier niño. Habiendo terminado: diseño gráfico, que aún ejerce profesionalmente, es inevitable que tenga varias ideas fijas sobre la imagen de bonsai. "Hoy en día, cada bonsai que creo debe de ser diferente - tan original como sea posible. No tengo un verdadero interés en seguir escrupulosamente los estilos japoneses, aunque si opino, que es una buena disciplina para aprender como fundamento."

Colin crée, que deberíamos de inclinarnos hacia las tendencias de nuestro arte y cultura autóctonos para de esta manera poder crear imagenes más evocativas y creativas." Después de todo, no tiene sentido el tratar de evocar imágenes de una tierra y cultura ajenas, ¿no es cierto?. Pero admite que hay una fuente de inspiración que es común en todos los entusiastas de bonsai - ese paisaje imaginario de la mente, donde todo es posible.

Siendo anteriormente miembro de la junta de la Asociación Europea de Bonsai, Colin Lewis ejerce en la actualidad, como asesor para la revista Bonsai en el Reino Unido, es miembro del jurado en el Chelsea Flower Show y autor de cuatro libros y un gran número de artículos para revistas. Da clases regularmente en su propio estudio y también en actos importantes por toda Europa y Los Estados Unidos de America.

Colin Lewis fait pousser des bonsaïs depuis vingt deux ans. Ses dix premières années furent consacrées au shohin. «Je ne savais pas quelle taille un bonsaï devait avoir» déclare-t-il. Pendant cette période, Colin devint compétent en toutes les techniques de base comme le rempotage, la taille, le ligaturage et dans une certaine mesure, le côté esthétique du bonsaï: «Je travaillais sur mes bonsaïs tous les soirs, et presque tous les week-ends. Cet entrainement constant assure l'arrivée naturelle des techniques, alors on ne s'en préoccupe plus – on peut se concentrer sur la forme et planifier les développements à venir.»

Colin Lewis est né en 1946 et fut élevé dans la campagne luxuriante du sud de l'Agleterre, un lieu où tous les garcons jouent régulièrement dans les arbres. Il fit des études de conception graphique. C'est sa profession aujourd'hui, alors, ce n'est pas étonnant qu'il ait des idées très définies sur les formes de bonsaï. «A présent, tout bonsaï que je crée doit être différent et aussi original que possible. Suivre servilement les formes Japonaises classiques ne m'intéresse plus, bien que je trouve important de m'être familiarisé avec ces styles.»

Colin croit qu'on doit puiser notre inspiration de notre héritage culturel et artistique, dans le but de créer des formes toujours plus imaginatives et évocatives. «Après tout, à quoi bon essayer d'évoquer des images d'un pays et d'une culture complètement étrangers?» Mais il admet quand même que tout est possible dans le paysage fantasque de l'esprit. Cette source d'inspiration est partagée par tous les amoureux de bonsaï.

Ancien membre du comité de l'Association Européenne de Bonsaï, Colin Lewis est à présent conseiller du Bonsaï magazine en Angleterre et juge au Chelsea Flower Show. Il est aussi l'auteur de 4 livres et d'un grand nombre d'articles de magazines. Il enseigne dans son atelier et aussi à des évènements à travers toute l'Europe et les Etats-Unis.

Colin Lewis gestaltet seit 22 Jahren Bonsai. Die ersten zehn Jahre davon hat er sich auf 'Shohin' konzentriert. Er behauptet für sich 'Ich hatte keine Ahnung' wie groß ein Bonsai sein soll. Während dieser Zeit eignete er sich Fähigkeiten in allen Basistechniken wie Umtopfen, Schneiden, Drahten und bis zu einem gewissen Grad der ästhetische Seite von Bonsai an. 'Ich pflegte fast jeden Abend und an den meisten Wochenenden an meinen Bonsai zu arbeiten. Diese dauernde Praxis bedeutet, daß die Techniken zweitrangig werden und man sich nicht mehr ausschließlich mit ihnen beschäftigt - man kann sich auf die Gestaltung konzentrieren und für die zukünftige Entwicklung planen'.

Colin Lewis wurde 1946 geboren und wuchs auf dem saftigen, grünen Land im Süden Englands auf. Er Studierte Graphik-Design und das ist auch heute noch sein Beruf. Daher ist es unvermeidlich, daß er einige ausgeprägte Ideen über Bonsai hat. 'Heute muß jeder Bonsai, den ich gestalte, unterschiedlich sein - so ursprünglich wie möglich'.

Ich habe keine Interesse mehr daran den klassischen japanischen Stilarten sklavisch zu folgen, obwohl ich der Meinung bin, daß es eine gute Lernmethode ist! Colin glaubt daß wir uns alle auf unser künstlerische und kulturelles Erbe besinnen sollen und stets Bäume mit einem imaginärem und beschwörenden Image gestlaten sollen 'Letzlich macht es doch keinen Sinn, Bilder von völlig fremden Ländern und Kulturen heraufzubeschwören, oder?'

Er läßt jedoch eine Inspirationsquelle zu, die alle Bonsailiebhabern gemeinsam haben - die phantastischen Landschaftes des Geistes, bei denen alles möglich ist. Colin Lewis ist ehemaliges Vorstandsmitglied der EBA und ist jetzt Berater des 'Bonsai Magazines' in Großbrittanien. Er ist Preisrichter bei der Chelsea Flower Chow und Autor von vier Büchern und ungezählten Artikeln in Bonsaimagazinen. Er unterrichtet regelmäßig in seinem eigenen Studio und bei großen Anlässen in ganz Europa und in den Vereinigten Staaten.

Colin Lewis
PO Box 317, West Byfleet,
Surrey KT14 6YG, United Kingdom.
Tel: +44 (0)1932 355455
Fax: +44 (0)1932 355880
E-mail: colin.s.lewis@btinternet.com

THE NAKED TRUTH

Many western bonsai artists I have spoken to express a preference for conifers, and some deny any interest at all in deciduous species. Perhaps this is a result of what I call the 'demonstration syndrome' – the pressure for rapid results. It is certainly widely influenced by the innovative work of Masahiko Kimura.

It could be said that, by specialising, the artist becomes more proficient in his chosen discipline and is therefore more able to challenge conventional artistic frontiers. On the other hand, there is always the danger that some aspects of bonsai may fall victim to fashion and become neglected or even disappear completely. Is it possible that the role of deciduous species in bonsai art could be under such a threat?

There is a clear distinction in mood and emotion between coniferous and deciduous bonsai – although neither is superior. But deciduous trees have an added dimension: the image profoundly changes each season, and with it the spirit also changes.

In spring, tiny buds burst to reveal minute, perfectly-formed leaves, like a baby's finger nails. The tree is vibrant with colour and full of promise. In summer, more heavily laden with foliage, deciduous bonsai are subject to more or less the same aesthetic criteria as conifers. In autumn we are rewarded by yet another change of character, this time a triumphant finale to the passing season.

But in winter the tree stands cold and naked, nothing can be hidden from view. The true souls of both the tree and its artist are exposed to the world's scrutiny.

Whether the tree is proud of its nakedness, or shamed by it, depends entirely on the competence and sensitivity of the artist. When displaying a conifer in winter the artist says, 'Look what I have done'. By displaying a deciduous bonsai in winter he also says, 'Look how I did it'.

With deciduous bonsai, therefore, branch structure is of paramount impor-

Colin Lewis

LA SCHIETTA VERITA

Molti artisti occidentalicon i quali ho parlato esprimono una preferenza per le conifere, ed alcuni negano qualsiasi interesse per le specie latifoglie. Può darsi che ciò è il risultano di quello che 'la sindrome delle dimostrazioni, la pressione per i risultati rapidi'. E' certamente un'influenza delle opere innovative di Masahiko Kimura.

Si potrebbe dire che tramite una specializzazione un artista diventa più esperto nella disciplina prescelta, ed è pertanto più capace a sfidare frontiere artistiche e convenzionali. D'altro canto esiste sempre il pericolo che certi aspetti del bonsai potrebbero subire, quali vittime della moda, e diventare trascurati oppure sparire del tutto. E' possibile che la specie delle latifoglie nell'arte bonsai potrebbe essere sotto una minaccia simile?

Esiste una chiara differenzza di umore ed emozioni tra bonsai di conifere e latifoglie, ma nessuno dei duo è superiore. La latifoglie hanno una dimensione in più: l'imagine cambia profondamente ogni stagione e con essa cambia anche lo spirito.

Nella primavera piccoli germogli appaiono e rivelano piccolissime foglie perfettamente formate come le unghie di un bambino. L'albero vibra di colore ed è pieno di promesse.

Nell'estate quando l'albero è appesantito dalle chiome, i bonsai di latifoglie mostrano gli stressi criteri estetici che conifere. In autunno ci regala un altro cambiamento di crattere, questa volta un finale trionfale per la stagione passata. Ma durante l'inverno, l'albero rimane freddo e nudo, niente è nascosto. Le anime vere, sia dell'albero, che dell'artista, sono completamente esposti allo scrutinio di tutti.

Se l'albero è fiero o si vergogna della sua nudità, dipende dalla competenza e sensibilità dell'artista. Quando mostra una conifera nell'inverno, l'artista dice 'Guardate ciò che ho fatto'. Mostrando una latifoglie d'inverno, dice 'Guardate come l'ho fatto'.

Con i bonsai di latifoglie, pertanto la

LA VERDAD DESNUDA

Muchos artistas de bonsai con los que he hablado, expresan una preferencia por las coníferas, y algunos niegan tener interés alguno en las especies caducifolias. A lo mejor este sea el resultado de lo que yo llamo "síndrome de demostracion" – la presión por los resultados rápidos. El está verdaderamente influenciado por el trabajo innovativo de Masahiko Kimura.

Podriamos decir que mediante la especialización, el artista se vuelve más competente en la disciplina elegida, y por lo tanto más capaz de superar el reto de nuevas barreras artísticas.

Por otro lado, siempre corre el peligro de que algunos aspectos del bonsai caigan víctimas de las diferentes modas, olvidándose e incluso desapareciendo completamente. ¿Es posible que el papel de las especies caducas en el arte de bonsai pueda estar bajo tal grave amenza?

Hay una clara distinción en el sentimiento y la emoción entre los bonsai coníferas y los caducifólios – aunque no podemos decir que unos sean superiores a los otros. Pero los árboles de hoja caduca poséen una dimensión adicional: la imagen profunda cambia con cada estación y con ella cambia también su espíritu.

En la primavera, diminutos capullos revelan delicadas hojas perfectamente formadas como las uñas de un recién nacido. El árbol es vigoroso con color y lleno de promesas. En verano, con el follaje profuso, el bonsai de hoja caduca está sujeto más o menos al mismo criterio que una conífera.

En otoño somos premiados aún, con otro cambio de carácter, esta vez un final triunfante a la pasada estación estival.

En el invierno el árbol se halla frío y desnudo, nada puede ser disimulado de la vista. La verdad, el alma de ambos, árbol y artista quedan totalmente descubiertos ante el escrutinio del mundo entero.

El que el árbol esté orgulloso de su desnudez, o avergonzado, depende integramente de la habilidad y sensibilidad del artista. Cuando se exhibe una conífera en invierno el artista dice: "Mirad lo que he creado". Al exhibir un bonsai caducifolio en invierno dice: "Mirad cómo lo he creado".

Con bonsais caducifólios por lo tanto, la estructura de su ramaje es de máxima

LA VÉRITÉ NUE

Beaucoup d'artistes de bonsaï occidentaux à qui j'ai parlé disent préférer les conifères et certains disent même n'avoir aucun intérêt pour les arbres à feuilles caduques. C'est peut-être le résultat de ce que j'appelle «le syndrome des démontrations». La pression pour les résultats rapides. Cette tendance est sûrement influencée par le travail pionnier de Masahiko Kimura.

On peut dire qu'en se spécialisant, l'artiste devient plus compétent dans sa discipline et devient ainsi capable de défier les frontières artistiques conventionnelles. D'une autre part, il est possible que certains aspects de l'art du bonsaï deviennent victimes de modes et soient négligées ou disparaissent même complètement. Le rôle des feuillus dans l'art bonsaï serait-il menacé?

L'état d'esprit et les émotions exprimés à travers les conifères et les feuillus sont très différents – bien que les uns ne soient pas supérieurs aux autres. Les feuillus ont une dimension de plus: leur image change profondément avec les saisons, et avec elle, leur âme change aussi. Au printemps, de petits bourgeons révèlent des feuilles minuscules et parfaites, comme des mains de bébé. L'arbre vibre de couleurs et est plein de promesses. En été, couverts de feuilles, les feuillus peuvents être jugés sur les mêmes critères que les conifères. En Automne, on est récompensé par un autre changement de personnalité, cette fois, une apothéose triomphante au passage des saisons.

Mais en hiver, l'arbre se tient droit, froid et nu, rien n'échappe au regard. L'âme vraie de l'arbre et celle de son artiste sont exposées à l'examen minutieux de tous.

Que l'arbre soit fier de sa nudité ou qu'il en ai honte dépend entièrement de la compétence et de la sensibilité de l'artiste. Quand il exhibe un conifère en hiver, l'artiste dit: «Regardez ce que j'ai fait.» Quand il montre un feuillu en hiver, il dit aussi: «Regardez comment j'ai fait.»

Avec les feuillus, la structure des branches est de la plus grande importance. Les branches placées sur des lignes peu

DIE NACKTE WAHRHEIT

Viele westliche Bonsaikünstler mit denen ich gesprochen habe, bekunden eine Vorliebe für Koniferen, andere lehnen jegliches Interesse für alle Laubbaumarten ab. Vielleicht ist dies das Ergebnis, dessen was ich als 'Demonstrationssyndrom' bezeichne - der Druck für schnelle Ergebnisse.

Man könnte sagen, daß der Künstler durch Spezialisierung in seiner geqählten Disziplin geübter wird und dadurch die konventionellen, künstlerischen Grenzen besser überschreiten kann. Andererseits besteht immer die Gefahr, daß dadurch manche Aspekte von Bonsai gewissermaßen zum Opfer fallen, daß sie nicht beachtet werden oder gar völlig verschwinden. Könnte es möglich sein, daß die Rolle der Laubbaumarten in der Bonsaikunst dedroht ist?

Zwischen Koniferen - und Laubbonsai besteht ein klarer Unterschied in den Stimmungen und Emotionen. Aber Laubbäume haben eine zusätzliche Dimension: das Erscheinungsbild ändert sich gründlich in jeder Jahreszeit und somit ändert sich auch das Wesen des Baumes.

Im Frühling brechen die Knospen auf und entfalten winzige, perfekt geformte Blätter, wie die Fingernägel eines Babys. Der Baum vibriert voller Farbe und Versprechen. Im Sommer, wenn sie mit Laub beladen sind, haben Laubbäume in etwa die gleichen ästhetischen Kriterien wie Koniferen. Im Herbst werden wir mit einem witeren Wechsel belohnt, jetzt ist es der triumphale Finale der zu Ende gehenden Jahreszeit.

Im Winter steht der Baum jedoch kalt und nackt da, nichts kann vor den Blicken verborgen werden. Die wahre Seele des Baumes und des Künstlers ist dem prüfenden Blick aller ausgesetzt. Ob der Baum stolz auf seine Nacktheit ist oder ob er sich schämt, hängt ganz von der Kompetenz und Sensitivität des Künstlers ab. Wenn ein Künstler eine Konifere im Winter ausstellt sagt er : 'Schaut, was ich getan habe' Wenn er im Winter einen Laubbaum ausstellt sagt er zusätzlich: 'Schaut, wie ich es getan habe'.

Die Aststruktur ist bei Laubbonsai daher

Ulmus procera

⬍ 45cm   ◁▷ 43cm

17 years / jahre / anni / ans / años

Seed / sämling / semina / graine / semilla

⬭ Walsall Studio

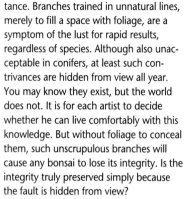

tance. Branches trained in unnatural lines, merely to fill a space with foliage, are a symptom of the lust for rapid results, regardless of species. Although also unacceptable in conifers, at least such contrivances are hidden from view all year. You may know they exist, but the world does not. It is for each artist to decide whether he can live comfortably with this knowledge. But without foliage to conceal them, such unscrupulous branches will cause any bonsai to lose its integrity. Is the integrity truly preserved simply because the fault is hidden from view?

Deciduous species also offer just as broad a range of images and emotions as those offered by conifers. The shapes may differ. The 'visual language' such as jin, shari, branch lines, colour and texture may change. But the image of an ancient oak, as old as time itself, tortured by centuries of attack, or a thrusting maple, vibrant with joyful vitality, can fill your heart, stir your soul and sing just as sweetly as any conifer.

Deciduous bonsai cannot be rushed. There is no formula for producing a seemingly established image in one session. Deciduous bonsai must be created slowly, a combination of vision, forward planning and adapting what nature presents each cycle. Branches must be built, year by year – each new shoot guided by wire until the entire network is complete. They become brittle at an early age, so once the work has been done it cannot be changed. The ghosts of mistakes made many years ago return each winter to haunt you.

The discipline of building branches in this way, the attitude of mind required to embark on a long-term project and, above all, the need for absolute integrity in your work, are all valuable lessons. Moreover, once learned, they serve to improve the integrity of all your bonsai, deciduous or coniferous.

struttura dei rami è di assoluta importanza. I rami impostati in linee non naturali, soltanto per riempire uno spazio con una chioma, sono sintomo di passione per i risultati rapidi, a prescindere dalla specie. Anche se quest è un metodo inaccettablie anche con le conifere, per lo meno i loro rami sono nascosti dalla vista tutto l'anno.

Sta all'artista decidere se può convivere con questa conscienza. Ma senza chioma per nascondere tali rami senza scrupoli, il bonsai perdarà tutta la sua integrità. L'integrità è conservata fino a quando l'errore è nascosto dalla vista. Le latifoglie offrono altrettante vaste scelte di immagini ed emozione, come le conifere.

Le forme posono essere diverse. 'Jin, shari, linee dei rami, colore e tessitura, possono cambiare, ma L'immagine di una quercia antica, vecchia come il tempo stesso, torturata da secoli di attacchi, o un acero sporgente, vibrante con gioisa vitalità, può riempirti il cuore, toccarti l'anima e cantare dolce come qualsiasi conifera'.

I bonsai di latifoglie non possono essere affrettati. Non esiste una formula per produrre un'apparente immagine stabila in una sola lavorazione. Le latifoglie devono essere create lentamente: una combinazione di visione, pianificazione anticipata, e l'adattamento di quella che la natura presenta ogni ciclo.

I rami devono essere construiti anno per anno ed ogni nuovo germioglio, guidato dal filo affinchè l'intera rete sia completata. Essi diventano molto fragile presto, quindi una volta compiuto il lavoro non possoro essere immediatamente cambiati. I fantasmi degli errori fatti negli anni precedenti tornano ogni inverno a pervadere l'animo del bonsaista.

La disciplina de construire rami in questa maniera, l'attidudine della mente richiesta per iniziare un progetto a lungo termine, e sopratutto il bisogno di assolutà integrità nel tuo lavoro, sono lezioni di grande valore. Inoltre, una volta imparati, servono a migliorare l'integrità di tutte le latifoglie o conifere.

importancia. Ramas modeladas con lineas innaturales, con el mero hecho de rellenar el espacio, ahora exento de hojas, es un síntoma de la codicia por los resultados rápidos, con una indiferencia total sobre la especie.

Aunque inaceptable con las coníferas, por lo menos tales estratagemas son difíciles de captar durante el año entero. Podemos adivinar su existencia, pero el resto del mundo no. Depende de la conciencia de cada artista, el poder vivir confortablemente con este conocimiento. Pero sin el follaje debido para poder camuflar estas peripecias, tales ramajes causarán la perdida de la integridad del bonsai ¿Está su integridad de veras preservada, al camuflar sus faltas a la vista humana? Las especies caducas ofrecen además una gama de imágenes y emociones tan amplia como esa de las coníferas. Las formas puede que sean diferentes. El "lenguaje visual" tal como jin, shari, líneas de las ramas color y texturas puede que varíen. Pero la imagen de un roble tan añejo como el tiempo mismo, torturado por siglos de ataques, o un arce agresivo, robusto, de vitalidad jubilosa, pueden colmar el corazón conmover el alma y cantar tan dulcemente como una conífera.

Los bonsais de hoja caduca no pueden ser apurados. No existe una fórmula que produzca una imagen de apariencia establecida con sólo una sesión. El bonsai caduco debe de crearse lentamente con una combinación de visualización previa, planificación y la adaptación de los ciclos naturales. Las ramas deben de ser construidas año tras año, cada brote guiado por medio del alambre, hasta que la cadena esté por fín completa. Ramas se vuelven quebradizas a una temprana edad, por lo tanto una vez concluido el trabajo, ya no puede ser alterado. Los fantasmas de los errores cometidos hace años, retornan cada invierno para perseguirnos.

La disciplina de la construcción de ramas de esta manera, la actitud mental necesaria para embarcar en un proyecto a largo plazo, y por encima de todo, la necesidad de una absoluta integridad en el trabajo individual, son lecciones de un valor incalculable. Por otra parte, una vez asimilado esto, nos servirá para mejorar la integridad de todos nuestros bonsais, sean caducos o coníferas.

naturelles, simplement pour emplir un espace avec du feuillage, sont les symptômes d'une soif de résultats rapides, quelques soit l'espèce d'arbre. Bien que ces techniques soient inacceptables même pour les conifères, au moins, sur ces arbres, elles sont cachées toute l'année. On sait qu'elles existent mais personne d'autre ne le sait. Chaque artiste doit décider par lui-même s'il est satisfait de vivre tout en sachant ce fait. Mais sans feuillage pour les cacher, ces branches sans scrupules entrainent la perte de l'intégrité de tout bonsaï. L'intégrité de l'arbre est-elle préservée simplement quand le défaut est caché?

Les arbres à feuilles caduques peuvent offrir un aussi grand choix d'images et d'émotions que les conifères. Les formes peuvent changer. Le language visuel exprimé par les jin, les shari, les lignes des branches, les couleurs et les textures peuvent changer. Mais l'image d'un chêne ancien, vieux comme le temps, torturé par des centaines d'années d'agression, ou un érable vigoureux, vibrant d'une vitalité joyeuse peuvent remplir nos coeurs, toucher nos âmes et chanter aussi agréablement que n'importe quel conifère.

Les feuillus ne doivent pas être précipités. C'est impossible de créer l' image d'un vieil arbre en une seule session. Les feuillus doivent être créés lentement, en pensant à l'avenir, en planifiant, et en adaptant tout ce que la nature nous offre à chaque saison. Les branches doivent être construites, tous les ans, chaque rameau guidé par des fils d'aluminium jusqu'à ce que toutes les ramifications soient en place. Les rameaux deviennent très vite cassants, dès lors, quand le travail est fini, il ne peut être changé. Le fantôme de toutes les erreures faites des années auparavant viendra vous hanter chaque hiver.

La discipline qui consiste à construire toutes les branches de cette façon, l'état d'esprit nécessaire pour s'embarquer sur un projet à long terme, et surtout, le besoin d'une intégrité totale dans son travail, sont toutes des leçons très utiles. De plus, une fois qu'on les a maîtrisées, elles servent à améliorer l'intégrité de tous nos bonsaïs; feuillus ou conifères.

von höchster Wichtigkeit. Äste, die in unnatürlichen Linien geformt sind und kaum einen freie Stelle mit Laub ausfüllen können, sind symptomanisch für die Lust auf schnelle Ergebnisse. Das gilt für alle Arten. Obwohl sie bei Koniferen auch nicht akzeptabel sind, sind solche 'Kunstgriffe' wenigstens das ganze Jahr nicht sichtbar. Sie wissen vielleicht selbst, daß sie existieren, aber die anderen wissen es nicht. Jeder Künstler muß selbst entscheiden ob er mit diesem Wissen gut leben kann. Aber wenn kein Laub diese gewissenlos gestaltete Aste mehr verbirgt, wird jeder Bonsai seine Integrität verlieren. Ist die Integrität wirklich bewahrt, wenn die Fehler den Blicken berborgen sind?

Die Laubbaumarten bieten eine genauso große Vielfalt an Erscheinungsbildern und Emotionen wie Koniferen. Die 'visuelle Sprache' wie beispielsweise Jin, Shari, Astverläufe, Farbe und Beschaffenheit können sich ändern. Aber das Erscheinungsbild einer uralten Eiche, so alt wie die Zeit selbst, gefoltert durch jahrhundertlange Attacken oder das eines Ahrons, das vor fröhlicher Vitalität vibriert, kann unsere Herzen erfüllen, unsere Seele rühren und ebenso süß singen wie eine Konifere.

Laubbäume müssen langsam gestaltet werden in einer Kombination aus Sehen, Vorausplanung und Anwendung dessen, was die Natur in jedem Zyklus präsentiert. Äste müssen Jahr für Jahr aufgebaut werden - jeder neue Trieb mit Draht in die richtige Position geführt werden, bis das ganze Netzwerk komplett ist. Äste werden schon zu einem frühen Zeitpunkt spröde, das heißt, daß sie später nicht mehr verändert werden können.

Die Disziplin mit der man auf diese Art und Weise Äste aufbaut, die notwendige Geisteshaltung, um sich auf ein Langzeit projekt einzulassen und vor allem die Notwendigkeit absoluter Integrität Ihrer Arbeit, sind alles wertvolle Lektionen. Darüberhinaus dienen sie dazu, wenn man sie einmal erlernt hat, gleichermaßen für Laubbonsai oder Koniferenbonsai.

◄ **Ulmus procera**

⇕ 40cm ◁▷ 42cm

± 40 years / jahre / anni / ans / años

Yamadori 1987

▭ Japan

▲ **Juniperus media x blaauwii**

⇕ 68cm ◁▷ 65cm

± 20 years / jahre / anni / ans / años

Tanuki 1986

▭ Bryan Albright

Alnus glutinosa

↕ 75cm ◁▷ 63cm

15 years / jahre / anni / ans / años

Seed / sämling / semina / graine / semilla

⌡ Walsall Studio

Salvatore Liporace

Salvatore Liporace, born in Belvedere Marittimo, Italy, is a professional bonsai artist. He established the "Studio Botanico" in Milan, the first place in Italy entirely dedicated to bonsai. Thanks to frequent meetings in Japan with his Master, Masahiko Kimura, his school has become a point of reference in Europe. Many of his students are affirmed teachers in Italy.

Two members of his school participated with success at the European Bonsai Association's New Talent Contest.

In Italy, he participates in radio and television programmes, demonstrations and workshops, making and has become known as an outstanding artist, confirming this with the publication of numerous articles in European and American magazines.

He is presently an official demonstrator at the most important European congresses, where his personal interpretation makes him one of the most requested professionals in Europe.

Salvatore Liporace, nato a Belvedere Marittimo (CS) Italia, è un artista bonsai professionista, fonda lo Studio Botanico in Milano (Italia), primo spazio interamente dedicato al bonsai. Grazie ai frequenti incontri in Giappone con il suo Maestro Masahiko Kimura la sua scuola diventa un punto di riferimento per l'Europa. Molti dei suoi studenti sono affermati istruttori in Italia.

Due membri della sua scuola hanno partecipato con successo al 'Nuovo Talento Europeo EBA'.

In Italia tiene rubriche radiofoniche e televisive oltre a dimostrazioni e workshops affermandosi come artista emergente; consolida il suo nome con la pubblicazione di numerosi articoli sulle più importanti riviste Europee ed Americane ed è presente come dimostratore ufficiale nei principali congressi Europei, dove la sua personale interpretazione dell'arte bonsai ne fa uno dei più richiesti dimostratori professionisti d'Europa.

▶ **Pinus mugo**
⇕46cm
± 160 years / jahre / anni / ans / años
Yamadori
⌷ China

Salvatore Liporace, nacido en Belvedere Marittimo, Italia, es un artista profesional de bonsai. El inaguró el 'Estudio Botánico' en Milán, el primer lugar en Italia enteramente dedicado al bonsai. Gracias a las frecuentes reuniones en Japón con su maestro, Masahiko Kimura, su escuela se ha convertido en un punto de referencia en Europa. Muchos de sus alumnos son ahora consolidados profesores en Italia.

Dos miembros de su escuela participaron con gran éxito en la competición de Talento Nuevo de la Asociacion Europea de Bonsai. En Italia, Salvatore participa en programas de televisión y radio además de demostraciones y talleres y ahora es reconocido como un artista muy destacado, ratificando esto con la publicación de numerosos artículos en revistas europeas y americanas.

El es actualmente demostrador oficial en los congresos europeos más importantes, donde su interpretación personal, le hace uno de los profesionales más solicitados de Europa.

Salvatore Liporace, né a Belvedere Marittimo, Italie, est un professionnel dans l'art du bonsaï, fonde le Studio Botanico à Milan, premier espace entièrement consacré au Bonsaï. Grace à de fréquentes recontres au Japon avec son Maitre Masahiko Kimura son école devient un point de repère pour l'Europe. Plusieurs étudiants de M. Liporace sont aujourd'hui des instructeurs affirmés en Italie.

Deux membres de l'école ont participé avec succès au concours "Nouveau Talent Européen EBA".

En Italie M. Liporace anime des émissions radio et télévisées, se prête à des démonstrations et des workshops, et s'affirme comme artiste émergent, il consolide sa renommée avec la publication de nombreux articles sur les revues européennes et amériacaines et partecipe en tant que démonstrateur officiel des principaux congrès européens où son inlerprétation personelle de l'art du Bonsai en fait un des démonstrateurs professionel en Europe les plus demandés.

Salvatore Liporace, der in Belvedere Marittimo, Italien, geboren wurde, ist ein professioneller Bonsaikünstler. In Mailand richtete er das 'Studio Notanico' ein, die erste Lokalität in Italien, die nur Bonsai gewidmet ist. Dank häufiger Treffen mit seinem Meister Mashiko Kimura, wurde seine Schule ein Beziehungspunkt in Europa. Viele seiner Studenten sind in Italien anerkannte Lehrer.

Zwei Mitglieder Seiner Schule nahmen erfolgreich an 'Neuen Taltentewettbewerb' der European Bonsai Association (EBA) teil. In Italien nimmt er bei Radio- und Fernsehe programmen teil. Er gibt Demonstrationen und Workshops. Er wurde als hervorragender Künstler bekannt, was durch die Veröffentlichung Zahlreicher Artikel in europäischen und amerikanischen Magazinen belegt ist.

Zur Zeit ist er offizieller Demonstrator bei den wichtigsten europäischen Kongreßen. Seine persönlichen Interpretationen machen ihn zu einem der meistgefragten Professionellen in Europa

STUDIO BOTANICO

Salvatore Liporace

Studio Botanico, Via Rubens 9,
20148 Milan, Italy
Tel: +39 (0)2 40 45 565
Fax: +39 (0)2 40 45 565

◀ **Juniperus 'San Jose'**
⇕ 50cm
± 80 years / jahre / anni / ans / años
Nursery / baumschule / vivaio / pépinière / vivero 1989
▭ Tokoname

Salvatore Liporace

BONSAI, SPIRIT AND SUBSTANCE

Let's now imagine a bonsai, caressed or beaten by the wind. Its slim trunk bends, following the invisible lines of force and gently opposing them, without ever surrendering. Over time, the side of the trunk facing towards the wind gets stronger and thickens. The part inside the curve buckles up until the bark comes off. And so the branches follow the ripples of the air which makes their leaves vibrate.

All this takes place without the plant knowing it. What counts is our thoughts which associate with the bonsai and mingle with it. Likewise it is our thoughts and hands which modify the tree.
The tree, changing, influences our thoughts and enters into our hearts. It is both the mirror of the soul of who looks after it and also part of his mind.

In these particular times, when the massacres of wars weigh heavily upon us like a terrible guilt, to speak about bonsai might seem like a way of escaping into a beautiful world, in order not to see, even to forget.

Once again the bonsai also reflects the soul of the person who made it. For the

BONSAI SPIRITO E MATERIA

Immaginiamo un bonsai accarezzato o frustato dal vento, vediamo il suo tronco esile piegarsi, accompagnando le invisibili linee di forza, opponendosi gentilmente senza mai cedere. Col tempo, la parte del tronco rivolta verso il vento si rafforza, si inspessisce; la parte interna alla curvatura si raggrinzisce fino a scortecciarsi: i rami inseguono anch'essi il fruscio dell'aria che fa vibrare la loro vegetazione.

Tutto ciò senza che la pianta sappia quello che fa, ma questo non nega la poeticità di una forma ventosa, perche quel che conta sono i nostri pensieri che si associano al bonsai e si proiettano su di esso. Così i nostri pensieri e le nostre mani modificano l'albero e l'albero, cambiando, influisce sui nostri pensieri ed entra nei nostri cuori. Esso è insieme specchio dell'anima di chi lo accudisce e parte della sua mente.

In questo momento in cui i massacri della guerra pesano su di noi come una colpa orrenda, parlare di bonsai può sembrare un modo di rifugiarsi in un mondo di bellezza per non vedere e per dimenticare, ma anche in questo il bonsai

BONSAI, ESPIRITU Y SUSTANCIA

Imaginémonos ahora un bonsai, a merced del viento. Su tronco delgado se corvará, siguiendo las lineas invisibles de las fuerzas, a la vez que suavemente las resistirá, para nunca subyugarse. A lo largo del tiempo, la parte del tronco que daba su cara al viento se vuelve más recia y más gruesa. La parte curva se deforma hasta que la corteza da de sí para luego desprenderse.

Todo esto ocurre sin la planta saberlo. Lo que cuenta son nuestros conceptos que se asocian con el bonsai hasta entremezclarse. Asimismo son nuestras ideas y manos las que modificarán el árbol. El árbol al cambiar, influye en nuestros pensamientos hasta adentrarse en nuestros corazones. Siendo por una parte el espejo del alma de su 'modelador' y por otra, parte de su mente.

En estos tiempos tan particulares, en los que las masacres de guerras civiles infunden cierta culpabilidad en todos nosotros, hablar de bonsai parecerá por lo tanto una forma de escapismo hacia un mundo hermoso, para así no ver e incluso olvidar.

Una vez más, el bonsai tambien refleja

BONSAI ESPRIT ET MATIERE

Imaginons un Bonsai caressé, fouetté par le vent, son tronc fragile se plie, accompagne d'invisibles lignes de force, s'oppose doucement sans jamais céder. Le temps passe, la partie du tronc face au vent se renforce, s'épaissie, la partie inférieure de la courbure se retrécie et puis s'écorche: les branches aussi suivent le bruissement de l'air qui fait vibrer leur végétation, la plante nous livre, sans le savoir, toute la poésie d'une forme au caractére venteux car ce qui compte c'est nostre ame qui s'unie au bonsaï et la projection de notre imaginaire.

Ainsi notre âme et nos mains modifient l'arbre, et l'arbre, tout en changeant, influence notre esprit et entre dans no coeurs. Il est à la fois un reflet de l'âme et une partie de l'esprit de celui qui le soigne. En ce moment parler de l'art du bonsaï, alors que les massacres de la guerre pèsent lourdement sur nous comme une horrible faute, peut sembler un moyen de se réfugier dans un monde de beauté permettant de ne rien voir et d'oublier, mais là aussi le bonsaï reflette l'âme de celui qui le fait.

BONSAI - GEIST UND SUBSTANZ

Lassen Sie uns einen Bonsai vorstellen, der vom Wind liebkost oder geschlagen wird. Sein schlanke Stamm biegt sich, die unsichtbaren Linien der Gewalt folgend. Er wehrt sich sanft dagegen, ohne je aufzugeben. Mit der Zeit wird die Seite des Stammes, die dem Wind zugeneigt ist, stärker und dicker. Die Innenseite biegt sich bis sich die Borke löst. Auch die Äste folgen dem Gekräusel der Luft, welches die Blätter vibrieren läßt.

Alle dies findet statt, ohne daß die Pflanze es weiß. Was zählt sind unsere Gedanken, die sich mit der Pflanze verbinden und sich mit ihr vermischen. Es sind auch unsere Gedanken und Hände, die den Baum andern. Der Baum verändert sich, beeinflußt unsere Gedanken und dringt in unsere Herzen ein. Es ist sowohl Spiegel der Seele als auch Teil des Verstandes dessen, der sich um den Bazn kümmert.

In diesen Zeiten, wo Massaker in Bürgerkriegen wie eine schwere Schuld auf uns zu lasten scheint, ist es wie eine Flucht in eine schöne Welt, wenn man über Bonsai spricht, damit man nicht hinschauen muß, ja damit man vergessen kann.

Noch einmal: Der Bonsai reflektiert die Seele dessen, der ihn gestaltet hat. Für die

superficial it may seem a hypocritical way of hiding. Those who approach it without depth, or haven't the inner serenity necessary to set a plant, will either obtain a tormented form or, more simply, by giving it an elegant, balanced and calm form will only stimulate, by contrast, his awareness that to pretend not to see, but simply to reflect and to pray isn't sufficient to cancel this crime against humanity and doesn't lighten the guilt of having been indifferent for too long and perhaps even being so today.

riflette l'anima di chi lo fa.

Per chi è superfficiale sarà un nascondersi ipocrita, chi si avvicina ad esso con profondità o non sentirà in se la serenita necessaria per impostare una pianta o otterrà una forma tormentata oppure, più semplicemente, dando a esso una forma elegante, equilibrata, serena, non farà che acuire, per contrasto, la sua consapevolezza che far finta di non vedere, riflettere, pregare, non basta a cancellare questo crimine contro l'umanità e non allevia la colpa di essere stati indifferenti troppo a lungo e forse di esserlo tuttora.

el alma de la persona que lo realizó. Para el superficial, debe de semejarse esto a una manera hipócrita de esconderse. Esos que se acerquen a este campo sin profundidad, o sin la serenidad necesaria para sembrar una planta, conseguirán por lo tanto una forma lobrega o al darle una forma elegante, equilibrada y calma simplemente estimulará, por contraste su conocimiento para pretender, no ver y con simplemente reflexionar y rezar no será suficiente para borrar su crimen contra la humanidad y no disculpa de haber sido indiferente durante tanto tiempo, o incluso aún seguir siéndolo.

Pour certaines personnes superficielles ce sera une façon hypocrite de se cacher, pour tous les autres, ceux qui approcheront cet art de plus prés, ceux qui n'auront pas la sérénité nécessaire permettant de créer une plante, ceux qui obtiendront une forme tourmentée ou enfin plus simplement, un forme élégante, équilibrée et sereine, ne feront qu'aviver par contradiction leur prise de conscience: ne pas ouvrir les yeux, ni réfléchir, ni prier ne suffit pas pour effacer ce crime contre l'humanité et ne soulage pas la faute d'avoir été indifférents trop longtemps et de l'être peut-être encore.

Oberflächlichen mag es ein heuchlerischer Weg sein, sich zu verstecken. Diejenigen, die ohne Tiefgang an die Sache gehen oder die, die nicht die innere Ruhe haben, eine Pflanze zu gestalten, werden entweder nur eine gequälte Form hervorbringen, oder einfacher gesagt, wenn man den Bonsai eine elegante ausgeglichene, ruhige Form gibt, wird man nur Aufmerksamkeit für das Wesentliche vortäuschen, ohne wirklich zu sehen.

Einfach nur in Betracht ziehen und beten reicht nicht aus dieses Verbrechen gegen die Menschlichkeit zu annulieren. Es verringert auch nicht die Schuld, zu lange gleichgültig gewesen zu sein und sogar heute noch zu sein.

Picea excelsa
⇕ 65cm
± 90 years / jahre / anni / ans / años
Yamadori
⌒ Japan

Chamaecyparis pisifera
⇕ 68cm
± 60 years / jahre / anni / ans / años
Nursery / baumschule / vivaio /
pépinière / vivero
⌒ Tokoname

Taxus cuspidata

⇕ 53cm ◁▷

± 60 years / jahre / anni / ans / años

Nursery / baumschule / vivaio /
pépinière / vivero

⬭ Tokoname

Juniperus rigida

⇕ 92cm

± 200 years / jahre / anni / ans / años

Yamadori

⬭ Tokoname

Marc Noelanders

Born in Belgium in 1960, Marc Noelanders was first introduced to the art of bonsai at the age of 21, during a seven-month stay in Japan, studying Japanese culture. On returning to Belgium, he began to study the Japanese language, which he now speaks and writes fluently.

Marc began to work with container-grown nursery material and became known as a specialist in this area. During an exhibition in Bruges, he was acclaimed for being 'very recognisable in his own personal and exceptional style'. Following this, he was invited to demonstrate first in the Netherlands, and then in Germany, Italy, France and Spain, as well as other locations.

Marc returned to Japan for extended stays in 1987 and 1989, on both occasions to study bonsai culture and techniques with teacher S. Sakurai. He discovered that the Japanese way of working is quite different from that practised in the west. In a Japanese bonsai nursery one works, without exception, for seven days a week and for at least twelve hours a day!

Having taken the decision to work full-time as a bonsai artist in 1990, Marc returned to Japan, this time to concentrate specifically on maintenance and re-styling techniques. From that moment onwards, his work gained the respect of the Japanese masters.

Marc made two more trips to Japan – in 1992 to study with H. Suzuki and in 1993 to assist Masahiko Kimura with his workshops.

Now an established bonsai professional, Marc Noelanders teaches bonsai to an ever-increasing number of groups, conducts workshops and demonstrations all over Europe, as well as Russia and the USA, and is responsible for maintaining major private collections such as that of Belgian Queen Paola, The Heidelberg Bonsai Museum and others.

Nato in Belgio nel 1960, Marc Noelanders fu introdotto all'arte bonsai all'età di 21 anni, durante un soggiorno di sette mesi in Giappone mentre studiava cultura giapponese. Una volta ritornato in Belgio ha iniziato ad imparare la lingua giapponese ed ora la parla e la scrive fluentemente.

Marc ha iniziato a lavorare su materiali da vivaio ed è rinnomato per essere uno specialista in questo tipo di lavorazioni. Durante un'esposizione, anni fa, a Bruges riscosse un notevole successo, raccogliendo numerevoli consensi, gli venne riconosciuto uno stile molto personale e di eccezzionale qualità.

Dopodiche fu invitato a tenere delle dimostrazioni nei Paesi Bassi, e successivamente in Germania, Italia, Francia e Spagna nonchè altri paesi.

Marc è tornato in Giappone per lunghi periodi nel 1987 e 1989, in tutte e due i casi per studiare cultura e tecnica bonsai con il maestro S. Sakurai. In un giardino bonsai in Giappone,si lavora, senza dubbio non meno di sette giorni alla settimana, dodici ore al giorno! In questi periodi di studio scoprì che i giapponesi lavorano in un modo assai diverso da quello occidentale.

Nel 1990 Marc divenne un bonsaista professionista. Il suo lavoro acquisì il rispetto dei maestri Giapponesi, quando tornò in Giappone per approfondire la conoscenza delle tecniche di mantenimento e modellazione.

Marc ha effettuato due altri viaggi in Giappone – nel 1992 per studiare con H. Suzuki e nel 1993 per assistere Masahiko Kimura in alcune sue dimostrazioni.

Ora Marc Noelanders è un professionista affermato di bonsai ed insegna a gruppi sempre più numerosi, tiene dimostrazioni dappertutto: Europa, nonchè Russia e in USA ed è responsabile del mantenimento di alcune importanti collezioni private fra le quali quella della Regina Belga Paola, del Heidelberg Bonsai Museum ed altre.

Taxus baccata

↕ 97cm ◁▷ 90cm

± 60 years / jahre / anni / ans / años

Nursery / baumschule / vivaio / pépinière / vivero 1991

⬡ Tokoname

Nacido en Bélgica en 1960, Marc Noelanders fué primeramente introducido al arte del bonsai a la edad de veintiún años, durante su estancia de siete meses en Japón, estudiando la cultura japonesa. A su regreso a Bélgica comenzó a estudiar japonés, lengua que actualmente habla y escribe con fluidez.

Marc empezó a trabajar con plantas de invernadero y se convirtió en un especialista en la materia. Durante una exposición en Brujas, fué aclamado por ser 'muy notable por su estilo propio y excepcional'. Seguidamente, fué invitado para demostrar primero en Holanda y luego en Alemania, Italia, Francia y España además en otros paises.

Marc volvió a Japón durante largas temporadas en 1987 y 1989, y en ambas situaciones para estudiar la cultura bonsai y sus técnicas con el maestro S. Sakurai. El descubrió que el método japonés es muy diferente del practicado aquí en occidente. En un taller de bonsai japonés se trabaja sin excepción, durante siete dias a la semana y por lo menos ¡doce horas al dia!

Habiendo tomado la decisión de ejercer en plena dedicación como artista de bonsai en 1990, Marc, volvió a Japón, esta ver para concentrarse específicamente en las técnicas de mantenimiento y re-estilización. De ahí en adelante, su trabajo obtuvo el reconocimiento de los maestros japoneses.

Marc regresó dos veces más al Japón – en 1992 para estudiar con H. Suzuki, y un año mas tarde para asistir a Masahiko Kimura con sus talleres.

Establecido en la actualidad, como un profesional de bonsai, Marc Noelanders enseña bonsai a un ascendente número de grupos, dirige talleres y demostraciones por toda Europa además de Rusia y Norte América y a su vez es responsable del mantenimiento de grandes colecciones privadas como la de la reina Paola de Bélgica y el Museo de bonsai de Heidelberg, entre otras.

Marc Noelanders est né en Belgique en 1960. Il fut introduit à l'art bonsaï à l'âge de 21 ans, lors d'un séjour de 7 mois au Japon, pour étudier la culture Japonaise. Quand il revint en Belgique, il commença à étudier la langue Japonaise, qu'il parle et écrit maintenant couramment.

Marc commença à travailler sur des arbustes de pépinières en pots et devint très vite connu pour être un spécialiste dans cette branche. Pendant une exposition à Bruges, on le proclama être un artiste remarquable pour son style très personnel et exceptionnel. Après, il fut invité à prendre part à des démonstrations aux Pays Bas, puis en Allemagne, en Italie, en France, en Espagne ainsi que dans plusieurs autres pays.

Marc retourna au Japon pour de longs séjours en 1987 et 1989, et à chaque fois, il étudia les techniques de bonsaï avec son professeur S Sakurai. Il découvrit que la façon dont les Japonais travaillent est très différente de celle pratiquée en occident. Dans une pépinière à bonsaï au Japon, on travaille sans exception sept jours par semaine et au moins douze heures par jour!

En 1990, Marc prit la décision de travailler à plein temps comme artiste à bonsaï, et retourna au Japon, cette fois pour se concentrer spécifiquement sur l'entretien et les techniques pour re-styliser un arbre. A partir de cette période, il gagne le respect des maîtres Japonais.

Marc fit encore deux autres voyages au Japon – en 1992 pour étudier avec H Suzuki et en 1993 pour assister Masahiko Kimura dans ses ateliers.

Il est dorénavant reconnu comme un professionel du bonsaï et enseigne l'art bonsaï à de plus en plus de groupes. Il mène des ateliers et donne des démonstrations à travers toute l'Europe ainsi qu'en Russie, aux USA, et est aussi responsable de l'entretien de grandes collections privées comme celle de la reine Paola de Belgique, celle du musée Heidelberg et bien d'autres.

Marc Noelanders wurde 1960 in Belgien geboren. Mit 21 Jahren, während eines siebenmonatigen Aufenthaltes in Japan, wo er die japanische Kultur studierte, hatte er den ersten Kontakt mit der Bonsaikunst. Nach Belgien zurückgekehrt, erlernte er die japanische Sprache, die er nun fließend spricht und schreibt.

Marc fing mit Baumschulmaterial an zu arbeiten und wurde dafür als Spezialist bekannt. Während einer Ausstellung in Brügge wurde er lobend hervorgehoben als jemand der 'seinen eigenen, außerordentlichen Stil hat'. Danach wurde er als Demonstrator zuerst in die Niederlande, danach nach Deutschland, Italien, Frankreich, Spanien und andere Länder eingeladen.

1987 und 1989 ging Marc wqieder für längere Zeit nach Japan. Beide Male studierte er dort bei seinem Lehrer S. Sakurai Bonsaikultur und-technik. Er fand heraus, daß die japanische Art zu arbeiten sehr unterschiedlich ist von der, die im Westen praktiziert wird. In einer japanischen Bonsaibaumschule arbeitet jeder, ohne Ausnahme, sieben Tage die Woche und mindestens zwölf Stunden am Tag!

Nachdem er 1990 die Entscheidung getroffen hatte, als Vollprofi als Bonsaikünstler zu arbeiten, ging Marc zurück nach Japan. Dieses Mal wollte er sich spezifisch auf die Pflege und Wiedergestaltungstechniken konzentrieren. Von diesem Zeitpunkt an wurde seine Arbeit von den japanischen Meistern geachtet.

Marc ging noch zweimal nach Japan, 1992 um bei H. Suzuki zu studieren, und 1993 um Masahiko Kimura bei dessen Workshops zu assistieren. Nun, da er ein etablierter Bonsaiprofi ist, lehrt Marc Bonsai einer stets wachsenden Anzahl von Gruppen. Er führt Workshops durch und gibt in ganz Europa, in Rußland und den USA Demonstrationen. Außerdem ist er für die Pflege von großen Privatsammlungen, wie z. b. der Sammlung der belgischen Königin Paola und des Heidelberger Bonsaimuseums verantwortlich.

Bonsai Art Noelanders

Luchtvaartstraat 7,
3500 Hasselt, Belgium
Tel: 0032 11 23 34 99
Fax: 0032 11 23 34 99

Marc Noelanders

NOTIONS OF JIN, SHARI AND SABAMIKI

These last few years driftwood has gained much in popularity, partially due to the creations of bonsai master Masahiko Kimura. When one has been occupied with bonsai for some time, one tends to long for more. When I first started bonsai a classical shape was considered the best and most beautiful. But after a few years I wanted to broaden my horizons and try to work more artistically. Bringing forward the artistic aspect is more difficult with deciduous trees, which is why there are more conifers in the collections of the masters, and driftwood, of course, is more suited to conifers.

Literally translated, jin means dead branch or top, sharimiki means peeled bark and sabamiki a hollow trunk. On wild potential bonsai collected from harsh environments, jin, shari and sabamiki are created by natural elements. These trees are called yamadori and are often of considerable age. The limited space and, sometimes, small amount of soil in which they grow keeps them small. Hail, avalanches, lightning and snow create the capricious forms and the areas of deadwood. However, we can create this deadwood artificially in our bonsai.

Please remember that one does not create dead wood features in a bonsai without function or reason. So why do we create jin, shari and sabamiki? Some good reasons are: to prevent rotting, to express a feeling of age, to camouflage or eliminate wounds, to give a tedious trunk more character or to thin and bend heavy branches and trunks. These are points worth remembering. By using the wrong techniques, or through inexperience, one might easily make a tree look worse than it did before. The tree could be ruined or may even die.

Here are some basic tips which I am sure will help you achieve good results. They are all important points which one should never forget.
• The health of the tree is most important.

NOZIONI DI JIN, SHARI E SABAMIKI

Negli ultimi anni il legno morto è divenuto sempre più popolare, in parte grazie alle creazioni del maestro del bonsai Masahiko Kimura. Più tempo si dedica all' arte del bonsai e più se ne vorrebbe dedicare. Quando cominciai a interessarmi al bonsai, la forma classica era considerata essere la migliore e la più bella. Ma dopo alcuni anni sentii l' esigenza di allargare i miei orizzonti e di adottare uno stile più artistico. Con gli alberi decidui, mettere in risalto l' aspetto artistico è molto più difficile, e questo spiega perché le collezioni dei maestri contengono un numero maggiore di conifere e il legno morto, naturalmente, si adatta molto meglio alle conifere.

Tradotto letteralmente, jin significa ramo morto o cima morta, sharimiki vuol dire corteccia staccata dall' albero e sabamiki è un tronco vuoto. Negli esemplari naturali che racchiudono in sé il potenziale per diventare un bonsai e che sono raccolti in ambienti selvaggi, jin, shari e sabamiki sono le creazioni degli elementi naturali. Questi alberi sono chiamati yamadori e spesso sono molto vecchi. Lo spazio limitato e, talvolta, l' esigua area di terreno in cui crescono, mantengono naturalmente ridotte le dimensioni dell' albero. Grandine, slavine, fulmini e neve creano le forme capricciose e le zone di legno morto. Ma nel nostro bonsai il legno morto può essere creato artificialmente.

Non dimenticate che in un bonsai le decorazioni di legno morto hanno sempre una funzione o una ragione ben precise. Allora perché creiamo jin, shari e sabamiki? Ci sono ragioni molto valide: per evitare la decomposizione, per esprimere una sensazione di età, per mimetizzare o eliminare delle imperfezioni, per dare a un tronco anonimo una qualità estetica o per sfoltire e piegare rami e tronchi più pesanti. Questi sono tutti punti preziosi da ricordare. Se si utilizzano le tecniche sbagliate, o se non si ha l' esperienza sufficiente, è facile peggiorare l' aspetto di un albero. L' albero potrebbe essere rovinato per sempre o addirittura morire.

Questi sono alcuni suggerimenti molto

NOCIONES DE JIN, SHARI Y SABAMIKI

En estos últimos años pasados la madera de deriva o de playa, ha adquirido mucha popularidad, debido en parte a las creaciones de bonsai del maestro Masahiko Kimura. Cuando se ha estado ocupado con bonsai durante algún tiempo, uno tiende a aspirar a más. Cuando comencé por primera vez con bonsai, la forma clásica era considerada como la más bella y la mejor. Pero años después, quise ensanchar mis horizontes y tratar de trabajar de una forma más artística. Presentar el aspecto artístico es más difícil con arboles caducifolios, esta es la razón por la que abundan las coníferas en las colecciones de los grandes maestros, y madera de deriva, por supuesto, es más apropiada para coníferas.

Traducido literalmente, jin significa rama o copa muerta, sharimiki quiere decir corteza descubierta y sabamiki tronco hueco. En lo silvestre un posible bonsai es recogido de un medio ambiente hostil, jin, sharimiki y sabamiki son creados por los elementos naturales. Son estos árboles llamados yamadori y son normalmente de una edad considerable. El espacio limitado y en algunos casos el escasez de suelo en el que se desarrollan, les mantiene de un tamaño reducido. Granizo, avalanchas y nieve crean las formas caprichosas y las zonas de madera seca. De qualquier modo, también podemos crear madera seca artificialmente en nuestro bonsai.

Por favor, no nos olvidemos que una persona no crea estos rasgos sin ninguna razón o función. Y entonces ¿por qué creamos jin, shari y sabamiki? Algunas de las mejores razones son por lo tanto: la prevención de la proliferación de sus raices, la simulación de una cierta edad, para camuflar o eliminar cicatrizes y dar a un tronco tedioso más caracter o también para afinar y doblar ramas y troncos gruesos. Estos son puntos que merece la pena recordar. Usando las técnicas incorrectas, o con inexperiencia, uno puede fácilmente conseguir que un árbol esté peor de lo que estaba en un principio. El árbol puede quedar arruinado e incluso morir.

He aquí algunas de las ideas que estoy seguro le ayudarán a conseguir buenos resul-

QUELQUES NOTIONS DE JIN, DE SHARI ET DE SABAMIKI

Toutes ces dernières années, les techniques artificielles comme celles qui donnent l'apparence de bois mort, sont devenues très populaires. Ceci est du partiellement aux créations du maître à bonsaï Masahiko Kimura. Quand on travaille sur des bonsaïs depuis plusieurs années, on aspire à de nouvelles choses. Quand j'ai commencé l'art bonsaï, une forme classique était considerée comme la meilleure et la plus belle. Mais après quelques années, j'ai voulu élargir mes horizons et essayer de travailler plus artistiquement. Faire ressortir l'aspect artistique est plus difficile avec les feuillus, c'est pourquoi il y a plus de conifères dans les collections des grands maîtres, et les techniques donnant l'apparence de bois mort sont bien sûr beaucoup plus adaptées au style des conifères.

Traduit littéralement, jin veut dire branche ou cime morte, sharimiki veut dire écorce arrachée et sabamiki, tronc creux. Sur les sauvageons recueuillis dans des environnements hostiles, les jin, shari et sabamiki sont crées par les éléments naturels. Ces arbres s'appellent les yamadori et sont souvent très vieux. L'espace très limité où ils poussent et le fait qu'ils ont souvent très peu de sol, les conservent tout petits. La grêle, les avalanches, la foudre et la neige leur donnent des formes capricieuses et tuent le bois en certains endroits. On peut créer cet effet de bois mort artificiellement sur nos bonsaïs.

Rapellez-vous toutefois qu'on ne crée pas des effets de bois mort sur un bonsaï sans rime ni raison. Alors pouquoi créer des jin, des shari et des sabamiki? Voici quelques bonnes raisons: pour empêcher la pourriture, pour donner une impression d'âge, pour cacher ou éliminer des cicatrices, pour donner plus de personnalité à un tronc sans intérêt ou enfin pour affiner ou plier des branches ou des troncs trop épais. Voilà ce dont il faut se rappeler. Si on utilise de mauvaises techniques, ou si on'a peu d'expérience, on peut facilement rendre un arbre beaucoup plus laid qu'il ne l'était auparavent. L'arbre pourrait être abimé et même

ANSICHTEN ÜBER JIN, SHARI UND SABAMIKI

In den letzten Jahren hat totes Holz, teilweise verursacht durch die Arbeiten von Meister Masahiko Kimura, viel an Popularität gewonnen. Wenn sich jemand eine Zeitlang mit Bonsai beschäftigt hat, wird er dazu neigen, noch mehr zu wollen. Als ich mit Bonsai anfing, wurde der klassische Bonsai als bester und schönster angesehen. Aber nach einigen Jahren wollte ich meinen Horizont erweitern und versuchte mehr künstlerisch zu arbeiten.

Bei Laubbäumen ist es schwieriger den künstlerischen Aspekt voranzubringen als bei Koniferen. Darum sind in den Sammlungen der Meister mehr Koniferen vorhanden und totes Holz paßt natürlich besser zu Nadelbäumen.

Genau übersetzt bedeutet 'Jin' toter Ast oder tote Spitze. 'Sabamiki' bedeutet abgeschälte Borke und 'Sabamiki' bedeutet hohler Stamm. Bei potentiellen Bonsai, die in der freien Natur gesammelt wurden und unter rauhen Umweltbedingungen standen, wurden Jins, Sharis und Sabamikis durch Naturelemente gestaltet. Diese Bäume nennt man Yamadori. Oft haben sie ein stattliches Alter.

Der begrenzte Platz und manchmal auch die geringe Erde in der sie wuchsen, hat sie klein gehalten. Hagel, Lawinen, Blitze und Schnee haben die kapriziösen Formen und die Bereiche von totem Holz geschaffen. Aber wir sind auch in der Lage, dieses tote Holz bei unseren Bonsai künstlich zu schaffen.

Bedenken Sie, daß man tote Holzteile bei Bonsai nicht ohne Funktion oder Grund gestaltet. Warum gestalten wir also Jin, Shari und Sabamiki? Hier sind ein paar gute Gründe dafür: um das Verfaulen zu verhindern, um ein Gefühl von Alter zu vermitteln, um Wunden auszumerzen oder unsichtbar zu machen, um einem langweiligen Stamm mehr Charakter zu geben oder um dicke Äste und Stämme dünner zu machen oder zu biegen - das sind Punkte, an die man sich erinnern sollte.

Wenn jemand falsche Techniken anwendet oder wenig Erfahrung hat, kann dadurch ein Baum schlimmer als vorher sein. Der

It must be healthy and strong.
- One must follow the lines on the trunk as closely as possible because these mark the flow of the sap. To interrupt the sap flow may cause the death of some branches.
- Examine the bark around old pruning wounds because it is possible that the cambium layer may have receded beneath the bark. Extra care is needed when creating shari in these cases.
- Examine the root ball in comparison with the remaining branches – their thickness, volume and placement
- What kind of bark does the tree have? With thin bark the cambium layer grows slower than with thick bark.
- When creating sabamiki, make sure that there is no possibility of water remaining in the wound, otherwise the deadwood may decay.
- It is very important to remember when making shari that the lifeline must be visible from the front of the tree. If not, one may get the impression of looking at a dead tree. The lifeline and foliage masses provide beautiful contrast with the driftwood.
- The areas of the living and dead parts of the tree must not be equal.

Last, but not least, when creating jin or shari, remember to do this at different points on the tree and not concentrated in one place. When a tree has very weathered, old bark with shari, it looks more natural to allow a jin to shine through the branches here and there.

A book could be written on this topic alone, especially when also considering the creative aspects. So let's always keep the following in mind: Never be satisfied too soon, because contentment is the enemy of creativity.

semplici che vi aiuteranno a raggiungere buoni risultati. Sono tutti punti importanti da non dimenticare.
- La salute dell' albero è la cosa più importante. L' albero deve essere sano e robusto.
- Seguite le linee del tronco il più fedelmente possibile perché queste segnano il flusso della resina. Interrompere il flusso della resina potrebbe causare la morte di alcuni rami.
- Esaminate la corteccia intorno ai segni di precedenti potature perché è possibile che lo strato di cambio sia receduto sotto la corteccia. Quando si crea lo shari in un caso come questo, è necessario essere molto prudenti.
- Esaminate le radici e confrontatele con il resto dei rami - il loro spessore, il volume e la posizione.
- Che tipo di corteccia ha l' albero? Con una corteccia sottile, lo strato di cambio cresce più lentamente rispetto alla corteccia più spessa.
- Quando si crea sabamiki, è importante accertarsi che nel punto dell' intaglio non ci sia acqua, altrimenti il legno morto potrebbe decomporsi.
- È importante ricordare che quando si crea uno shari, la linea della vita deve essere visibile dalla parte anteriore dell' albero. Se non fosse visibile, uno potrebbe avere l' impressione di ammirare un albero morto. La linea della vita e le masse delle foglie creano un meraviglioso contrasto con il legno morto.
- Le aree delle sezioni viventi e morte dell' albero non devono essere eguali.

E per finire, ma comunque sempre importante, quando si crea un jin o uno shari, ricordatevi di farlo in punti diversi dell' albero e di non concentrarli in un punto solo. Se nello shari un albero ha una corteccia molto vecchia e stagionata, potrete creare un effetto molto più naturale se lasciate che un jin appaia qua e là fra i rami.

Potrei scrivere un libro intero su questo argomento, soprattutto se si pensa ai suoi aspeti creativi. Cerchiamo di tenere sempre presente questo principio: È meglio essere sempre un po' scontenti, perché l' appagamento è il nemico della creatività.

tados. Son todos puntos importantes que nunca se deben de olvidar.
- La salud del árbol es muy importante. Debe de estar sano y fuerte.
- Deberemos de seguir las líneas del tronco lo más cerca posible porque estas últimas señalan la fluencia de la savia. La interrupción del movimiento de la sávia puede causar la muerte de algunas de sus ramas.
- Examinar la corteza circundante a las cicatrizes producidas por las diferentes podas ya que es posible que el cámbium o capa generatriz, haya disminuido bajo la corteza. Se requiere por lo tanto mucho cuidado al crear shari en estas circunstancias.
- Observar el tamaño global de la raiz en comparación con las ramas restantes – su grosor, volumen y posición.
- ¿Qué clase de corteza tiene el árbol?. Si es delgada el cámbium se desarrollará más lentamente que si esta última fuese gruesa.
- Al crear sabamiki, debemos de asegurarnos que no haya residuos de agua en las heridas, de otra manera la madera seca llegara a pudrirse.
- Es muy importante recordar cuando practicamos shari que la sustancia y viveza de la planta debe de ser visible desde la parte frontal del árbol. Si no fuera así nos daría la impresión de estar presenciando un árbol muerto. Su vitalidad y follaje proporciona un bello contraste con la madera seca.
- Las áreas vivas y muertas del árbol deben de ser desiguales.

Y por último, cuando se crea jin o shari, debemos de tener presente el hacerlo en diferentes partes del árbol, Y no concentrarnos en un punto concreto. Cuando un árbol ha sido curtido por las diferente condiciones metereológicas, la corteza antigua con shari parecerá más natural al lucir tambien un jin entre ramajes dispersos.

Se podria escribir in libro solo sobre este tópico, en especial considerando los aspectos creativos. Por lo tanto tengamos siempre en cuenta lo siguiente: Nunca debemos de estar satisfechos demasiado pronto, ya que la conformidad es el enemigo de la creactividad.

mourir. Voici quelques conseils de base pour vous aider à obtenir de bons résultats. Ce sont des conseils importants qu'il ne faut pas oublier.
- La santé de l'arbre est la chose la plus importante. Il doit être en bonne santé et pousser vigoureusement.
- Il faut suivre les lignes du tronc d'aussi près que possible parce que ces lignes sont suivies par la sève. Interrompre l'écoulement de la sève pourrait causer la mort de certaines branches.
- Il faut examiner l'écorce autour des vieilles cicatrices dues a l'élagage. Il est en effet possible que le cambium ai reculé jusqu'à se trouver sous l'écorce. Alors, il faut faire très attention si l'on veut créer un shari dans ce cas.
- Regardez bien la motte de racines en relation avec les branches qui restent – leur épaisseur, leur volume et leur emplacement.
- Quelle genre d'écorce l'arbre a-t-il? Si l'écorce est fine, la couche de cambium pousse moins vite que celle des arbres à l'écorce épaisse.
- Quand on crée des sabamiki, il faut s'assurer que l'eau de pluie ne peut pas stagner dans la blessure, ou alors le bois mort pourrait pourrir.
- Quand on crée un shari, il faut se rappeler que la ligne de vie doit être visible du devant de l'arbre. Si non, on aura l'impression de regarder un arbre mort. La ligne de vie et les coussinnets de feuillage forment un très beau contraste avec le bois mort.
- Les parties vivantes et les parties mortes de l'arbre ne doivent pas être de taille égale.

Enfin, quand on crée un jin ou un shari à un endroit, il faut en crèer à d'autres endroits sur la surface de l'arbre. Quand un arbre a une très vieille écorce marquée par les intempéries, un jin sortant des branches ici ou là, aura l'air plus naturel.

On pourrait écrire un livre sur le sujet; surtout si l'on tient compte aussi du côte créatif. Alors, il ne faut pas oublier qu'il ne faut pas être satisfait trop tôt, parce que la satisfaction est l'ennemie de la créativité.

Baum kann ruiniert werden und sogar sterben. Hier sind ein paar Grundratschläge, bei denen ich sicher bin, daß sie Ihnen zu besseren Ergebnissen verhelfen. Es sind wichtige Punkte, die man nie vergessen sollte.

• Man muß den Linien des Stammes so dicht wie möglich folgen - Diese Linien zeigen uns den Saftstrom. Wird der Saftstrom unterbrochen, kann das den Tod von einigen Ästen bedeuten.

• Prüfen Sie die Rinde an alten Schnittwunden. Es ist nämlich möglich, daß sich die Kambiumschicht unter der Rinde zurückgezogen hat. Bei der Gestaltung von Shari muß man in diesem Fall besonders vorsichtig sein.

• Überprüfen Sie den Wurzellballen im Vergleich zu den verbleibenden Ästen - ihre Dicke, ihr Volumen und ihre Anordnung.

• Welche Art von Borke hat der Baum? Bei dünner Borke wächst die Kambiumschicht langsamer als bei einer dicken Borke.

• Bei der Gestaltung von Sabamiki muß man sich vergewissern, daß kein Wasser in der Wunde verbleiben kann, sonst kann das tote Holz verfaulen!

• Wenn Sie Shari gestalten, ist es sehr wichtig sich daran zu erinnern, daß die Lebenslinie (Saftbahn) von vorne am Baum zu sehen ist. Sonst könnte man den Eindruck haben, einen toten Baum zu betrachten! Die Lebenslinie und das Laub stehen im schönen Kontrast zum toten Holz.

• Die lebenden und abgestorbenen Teile des Baumes sollten nicht gleich groß sein.

Als letzter, aber nicht als unwichtigste Punkt sollten Sie sich beider Gestaltung von Jin und Shari darüber im Klaren sein, daß sich diese nicht an der gleichen Stelle des Baumes befinden, sondern an verschiedenen Punkten. Wenn ein Baum eine sehr verwitterte, alte Borke mit Shari hat, sieht es natürlicher aus, wenn Jins hier und da durch die Äste hindurchscheinen. Allein über dieses Thema könnte man ein Buch schreiben, besonders wenn man auch die kreativen Aspekte berücksichtigt. So laßt uns immer folgendes bedenken: Man sollte nie zu früh zufrieden sein, denn Zufriedenheit ist der Feind der Kreativität.

Metasequoia glyptostroboides
↕120cm ◁▷ 68cm
± 40 years / jahre / anni / ans / años
Nursery / baumschule / vivaio /
pépinière / vivero 1989
⌐⌐ Tokoname

Picea glehnii

↕ 63cm ◁▷ 44cm

± 30 years / jahre / anni / ans / años

Nursery / baumschule / vivaio /
pépinière / vivero 1995

▭ Tokoname

▲ Pinus mugo
⇕ 58cm ◁▷ 83cm
± 60 years / jahre / anni / ans / años
Yamadori 1996
▱ Tokoname

▲ **Juniperus communis**

⇕ 44cm   ◁▷ 47cm

± 160 years / jahre / anni / ans / años

Yamadori 1994

▭ Tokoname

SWITZERLAND

Pius Notter

GB

When Pius Notter created his first bonsai from domestic trees in 1976, there were only a few people in Europe who knew anything about this Oriental art. He is justifiably considered to be a pioneer, especially in the use of yamadori - domestic wild trees. As founding member of various clubs and associations, eg. the European Bonsai Association and Vereinigung Schweizer Bonsai-Freunde (VSB), he deserves recognition for his strong involvement. He was honoured in 1991 by being appointed as 'Honorary President' of VSB.

Pius Notter's creations have received acknowledgement and praise throughout the world. He was the first, and so far the only European to be invited as a demonstrator at a world convention. The Nippon Bonsai Association award in 1988 can be considered one of the major milestones in his international demonstrator career.

In Japan he is considered the most appreciated foreign creator, reflected in his introduction as the first non-Japanese in the leading Kindai-Shuppan magazine. He was awarded prizes in the United States for his work. In 1994, he was awarded the 'Golden Membership' by Bonsai Clubs International, who honoured him again same year with the 'Writers and Photographers Award' in acknowledgement of his worldwide achievements. His 7 books are considered guidelines for the creation of bonsai. Some have been translated into several languages. He has also designed and built the Arboretum in Boswil, Switzerland, where he gives weekend seminars that are in high demand.

Over the past seven years, more than 100 students have created approximately 200 trees under his supervision. A large number can be admired at exhibitions throughout Europe. These students are the vehicle that spreads his creative design technique and philosophy continually in all directions. Through this method of proliferation, he is able to promote design quality and leave a lasting impression on the bonsai scene.

I

Quando Pius Notter ha realizzato nel 1976 i primi bonsai da specie arboree indigene, soltanto pochi in Europa conoscevano quest'arte orientale. Pertanto egli è giustamente considerato un pioniere, specialmente per quanto riguarda l'impostazione di piante raccolte in natura (yamadori).

Egli ha il grande merito di essere cofondatore di diversi club e associazioni, tra cui la European Bonsai Association (EBA) e l'Associazione Svizzera degli Amici del Bonsai (VSB). Per il suo forte impegno per la divulgazione dell'arte bonsai ha ricevuto nel 1991 la nomina a Presidente Onorario della VSB.

Presto le sue creazioni sono state conosciute ed apprezzate a livello mondiale. Nel 1988 è stato premiato per il suo lavoro dalla Nippon Bonsai Association. E' stato il primo e finora l'unico europeo, ad essere invitato al Congresso Mondiale come dimostratore-headliner. Da molti anni figura tra i dimostratori più richiesti a livello internazionale.

In Giappone Pius Notter è il dimostratore straniero più apprezzato. E' stato il primo dimostratore 'non-giapponese' ad essere presentato nel marzo del 1997 nella famosa rivista Kindai-Shuppan. Anche in America ha ottenuto lusinghieri successi per i suoi lavori. Nel 1994 il Bonsai Club International (BCI) gli ha conferito la 'Golden Membership'. Sempre nel 1994 il BCI lo ha onorato con l' ambito premio 'Writers and Photographers Award' come autore e fotografo per il suo lavoro in campo internazionale.

I suoi sette libri sullo specifico tema del bonsai sono ormai entrati a far parte della letteratura classica ed alcuni di questi libri sono stati tradotti in diverse lingue.

Egli è inoltre fondatore e realizzatore dell'Arboretum di Boswil, in Svizzera, dove durante i week-end si svolgono i suoi ambiti seminari. Negli ultimi sette anni più di cento studenti vi hanno partecipato, impostando oltre duecento alberi che oggi sono ammirati nelle mostre di tutta Europa. Grazie a questi giovani, la sua caratteristica tecnica di impostazione e la sua filosofia si diffondono in tutte le direzioni. Con il suo metodo Pius Notter contribuisce in maniera decisiva al miglioramento della qualità della impostazione in Europa, lasciando un' impronta duratura sulla scena bonsai.

Juniperus sabina
⇕120cm ◁▷ 90cm
Yamadori
▭ Tokoname

▲ **Picea abies**
↕ 75cm ◁▷ 75cm
Yamadori 1994
⬭ Tokoname

Cuando Pius Notter creó su primer bonsai de un árbol doméstico, en 1976, existía entonces un pequeño grupo en Europa que sabían algo referente a este arte del lejano oriente. Por lo tanto, él, se considera un pionero, en especial en el utilización de yamadori.

Como miembro fundador de varios clubs y asociaciones, como por ejemplo la Asociación Europea de Bonsai y Veirinigung Schweizer Bonsai-Freunde (VSB), Pius merece ser reconocido por su gran colaboración. Consiguientemente, fué honrado en 1991 con el título de "Presidente Honorario" del VSB.

Las creaciones de Pius Notter han logrado obtener reconocimiento y apreciación a través del mundo entero. Fué él, el iniciador, y hasta ahora el primer europeo que ha asistido como invitado especial en una convención mundial. Ser galardonado con el premio de la Asociación de Bonsai de Nippon puede considerarse como la cúspide de su carrera como demostrador internacional.

Los japoneses le consideran como el creador extranjero de más aprecio reflejandose esto último en su introducción como el primer no-japonés en la revista de bonsai de más importancia: Kindai-Shuppan. Le han sido a su vez otorgados premios en los Estados Unidos por su continuo trabajo. En 1994 el Bonsai Clubs International le premio con el "Golden Membership" y BCI le honró ese mismo año con el "Premio de Fotógrafos y Escritores" en reconocimiento por sus éxitos a nivel mundial como autor y fotógrafo.

Los siete libros de Pius Notter son considerados como pautas para la creación de bonsai. Varias de estas publicaciones han sido traducidas en diferentes lenguas. También ha sido diseñador y constructor del "Arboretum" de Boswill (Suiza), donde da seminarios de fines de semana con gran éxito.

Durante los pasados siete años, más de cien estudiantes han creado unos doscientos árboles bajo su supervisión. Un gran número de estos últimos, pueden ser admirados en diversas exhibiciones a través de Europa. Estos estudiantes son el vehículo con el que su diseño creativo, su técnica y filosofía, son propagados continuamente en todas las direcciones. Mediante este método de difusión, él es capaz de promocionar calidad en el diseño y dejar una impresión duradera en la escena de bonsai.

Lorsqu'en 1976 Pius Notter créa les premiers bonsaï à partir d'arbres indigènes, très peu de gens connaissaient cet art d'Extrème Orient. Pour cette raison il est considéré comme un pionnier du bonsaï et tout particulièrement dans la formation d'arbres prélévés (yamadori). En tant que cofondateur de différents clubs et fédérations, comme par exemple l'European Bonsai Association (EBA) et l'Association Suisse des Amis du Bonsaï (VSB), il acquiert une réputation. Il fut notamment pour cette raison nommé président d'honneur du VSB en 1991.

Ses créations ont obtenu très rapidement une reconnaissance au niveau mondial. une d'entre elles fut primée par la Nippon Bonsai Association. Il fut le premier et jusqu'à présent le seul européen à être invité comme démonstrateur vedette à un congrès mondial. Il est depuis de nombreuses années un démonstrateur apprécié et reconnu dans le monde entier. Il est considéré par les japonais comme le démonstrateur étranger le plus renommé. Le célèbre magazine Kindai-Shuppan le présenta en tant que créateur dans son édition de mars 1997, ce fut une première pour un non-japonais. Ces travaux furent aussi récompensés aux Etats-Unis où le Bonsai Club International le fit «Golden Membership» en 1994. Dans la même année le BCI lui décerna le «Writers and Photographers Award» en reconnaissance de son œuvre mondiale en tant qu'auteur et photographe. Les sept livres dont il est l'auteur sont considérés comme des éléments essentiels de la litterature sur le bonsaï. Ils ont été en partie traduits en sept langues.

Il est le créateur de l'arborétum de Boswil en Suisse où il y dirige les séminaires particulièrement très appréciés. Durant les sept dernières années, il a transmis par ce biais son savoir à plus de 100 élèves et réalisé avec eux plus de 200 arbres, lesquels sont très remarqués lors des expositions dans l'Europe entière. Au travers de ses élèves, ses techniques de création ainsi que sa philosophie ont trouvé un terrain de développement très intéressant. Ici il participe de façon très significative à l'évolution qualitative du bonsaï en Europe.

Als Pius Notter 1976 die ersten Bonsai aus einheimischen Bäumen gestaltete, wussten nur wenige in Europa über diese fernöstliche Kunst Bescheid. Er gilt deshalb mit Recht als Pionier und dies im speziellen in der Gestaltung von Wildpflanzen (Yamadori).

Als Mitgründer verschiedener Clubs und Vereinigungen, wie zum Beispiel die European Bonsai Association (EBA) und die Vereinigung Schweizer Bonsai-Freunde (VSB) hat er sich grosse Verdienste gemacht. 1991 wurde er deswegen geehrt und zum Ehrenpräsidenten der VSB ernannt.

Seine Gestaltungen ernteten schon bald weltweit grosse Anerkennung und 1988 wurde er für seine Arbeit von der Nippon Bonsai-Association ausgezeichnet. Als erster und bis heute einziger Europäer wurde er als headliner Demonstrator zum Weltkongress eingeladen. Er ist seit Jahren der begehrteste Demonstrator weltweit.

In Japan gilt er als der anerkannteste Gestalter ausserhalb Japans. Als erster Nicht-japaner wurde er im März 1997 im führenden Magazin Kindai-Shuppan vorgestellt.

Auch in Amerika hat man seine Arbeiten ausgezeichnet. 1994 erhielt er vom Bonsai Club International (BCI) die Goldmitgliedschaft. Im gleichen Jahr wird ihm der begehrte 'Writers and Photographers Award' als Anerkennung für seine weltweite Arbeit als Autor und Photograph verliehen.

Seine sieben Fachbücher gelten als die wegweisende Literatur zum Thema Bonsai-Gestaltung. Seine Bücher sind zum Teil in sieben Sprachen übersetzt.

Weiter ist er der Erbauer des Arboretums in Boswil in der Schweiz, wo er auch seine begehrten Wochenendseminare durchführt. In den letzten sieben Jahren hat er mehr als 100 Studenten gelehrt und mit ihnen fast 200 Bäume gestaltet, die heute überall in Europa an Ausstellungen bewundert werden. Seine spezielle Gestaltungstechnik und Philosophie wird somit wie durch ein grosses Netz immer weiter getragen. So trägt er massgeblich zur Steigerung der Gestaltungsqualität in Europa bei und prägt die Bonsai-Szene erheblich.

Pius Notter
Chäsiweg 3
5623 Boswil, Switzerland
Tel: 0041 56 666 24 20
Fax: 0041 56 666 12 92

Pius Notter

BONSAI

Unfortunately, bonsai is often considered to be a pure 'gardeners' product'. The Japanese and Chinese contribute to this image by styling little plants to resemble bonsai and exporting them by the hundreds of thousands. Pius Notter doesn't consider bonsai to be a gardener's product. In his opinion, bonsai means creative work, which demands knowledge of perspective, depth effects, harmony and shapes. It is a matter of course that the designer possesses a basic knowledge of plants and their growth cycles.

The whole creative work only makes sense if one knows exactly how to respect the life of the plant. It doesn't help to be a trained gardener without adequate creative talent, and vice versa. This means that bonsai is the result of creative work on a living plant and success is dependent upon multi-talent and knowledge.

I would like to show an example that demonstrates that the combination of plant knowledge and design leads to a fantastic, creative change in the plant. The work on the plant might eventually appear spectacular to an amateur. However, for the plant itself, it is a harmonious operation, which cannot be compared to the effects resulting from decades of exposure to the brutal forces of nature.

In mountain regions, with extreme climates, one can find a special juniper which is often marked by interesting jin and shari elements. Unfortunately, they often have long and thin trunks. The long trunk is sometimes out of proportion, thin, and lies flat on the ground. On the bottom of the trunk you can very often find the sap-stream, which is the only grain of life between the foliage and the roots that has not been damaged by snow, avalanches and landslides.

The original trunk was a lot more voluminous, before the forces of nature removed the bark on the upper side. The wood is now dead and bleached by the sun. The tree doesn't actually need this

BONSAI

Ancora troppo spesso il bonsai viene visto come puro prodotto del giardinaggio. A questa immagine contribuiscono le centinaia di migliaia di piantine prodotte in Cina e in Giappone e destinate all'export, "potate" per farne miniature simili a bonsai.

Io no considero il bonsai un prodotto del giardinaggio, ma principalmente il risultatodi una attivà creativa che richiede, oltre ad ampie conoscenze della natura e dei ritmi di crescita delle piante, anche cognizioni sulla prospettiva, sull'effetto di profondità e sull'armonia delle forme. Il lavoro creativo sulla pianta ha senso solo sapendo come salvaguardarne la vita. Per essere un bravo bonsaista non è sufficiente essere un esperto giardiniere, ma bisogna anche possedere talento artistico.

Bonsai è quindi il risultato di un lavoro creativo su una pianta viva e il successo si può raggiungere solo possedendo diversi talenti ed ampie conoscenze.

Vorrei quì dimostrare con un esempio come la combinazione tra la conoscenza delle piante e l'impostazione creativa porta alla stradordinaria trasformazione fi una pianta. A volte al profano questo lavoro può sembrare cruento, in verità si tratta di un intervento del tutto innocuo e non paragonabile alla 'brutalità' delle forze delle natura alla quale la stessa pianta è stata sottoposta per decenni.

In alcune regioni montane dal clima particolarmente avverso si possono trovare piante con interessanti parti di jin e shari, specialmente ginepri. Questi alberi sviluppano spesso un tronco sproporzionatamente lungo e sottile. Di frequente il tronco è appoggiato sulla terra; gli unici canali linfatici funzionali si trovano nella parte inferiore, che non è stata danneggiata da slavine e cadute di sassi. Il lato superiore del tronco, che in origine era molto più grosso, è stato Scorticato dalle forze della natura, il legno è morto e sbiancato dal sole. Si tratta quindi di una parte non più necessaria alla sopravvivenza

BONSAI

Desgraciadamente, bonsai está frecuentemente considerado como un producto "puramente" del horticultor. Los chinos y japoneses contribuyen a esta imagen, por su costumbre en estilizar plantas pequeñas que imitan bonsai, y son exportadas en cantidades masivas. Pius no considera bonsai como un producto enteramente del jardinero. En su opinión, bonsai significa el trabajo creativo que demanda conocimiento de perspectiva, efectos profundos, armonias y formas. Es un hecho palpable que el diseñador posée un conocimiento clave de las plantas y sus círculos vitales.

El trabajo creativo en conjunto, sólo tiene sentido si se sabe respetar la vida de la planta. No ayuda el que se sea un jardinero de gran experiencia, pero sin el talento creativo necesario o vice versa. Con esto quiero decir que bonsai es el producto del trabajo creativo en una planta viva y su éxito dependerá del talento y la sabiduría del diseñador.

Me gustaría mostrar un ejemplar,que demuestra precisamente la combinación de planta, conocimiento y diseño con el resultado de un cambio creativo y espectacular. El trabajo en el árbol posiblemente sea considerado como espectacular para el amateur. De todos modos para la planta esta es una operación armoniosa, la cual no puede ser comparada con los efectos resultantes de décadas de exposición a las fuerzas brutales de la naturaleza.

En las regiones montañosas, con sus climas extremos, podemos encontrar un junípero especial, el cual está frecuentemente marcado con interesantes elementos de jin y shari. Por desgracia, en muchos casos con el tronco demasiado largo y delgado. El tronco esta desproporcionado, débil y al ras del suelo. En la base del tronco, podemos encontrar muchas veces el flujo de la savia, el cual es el único "hilo" de vida entre las hojas y las raices y que no ha sido dañado por la intemperie.

El tronco original, debía de ser mucho

LE BONSAI

Le bonsaï est malheureusement considéré comme un produit du domaine de l'horticulture. Cela peut se comprendre lorsque l'on sait que pour le commerce de gros destiné à l'exportation on cultive au Japon et en Chine des centaines de milliers de petits arbres dits «bonsaï».

Pour moi le bonsaï n'est pas un produit d'horticulture. Je ne suis moi-même pas un jardinier et ni même botaniste. Le bonsaï est avant tout un art créatif qui nécessite des connaissances relatives à la perspective, à l'effet de profondeur et à l'harmonie des formes. Bien entendu il est nécessaire d'avoir des connaissances sur les végétaux et leur développement, car le travail créatif sur l'arbre n'a de sens, que si l'on sait garder l'arbre en vie. Pour cet art rien ne sert d'être un horticulteur averti si l'on n'a aucun sens créatif et inversement.

Le bonsaï est le résultat d'un travail créatif sur un végétal vivant. Un succès n'est possible que s'il y a combinaison du talent et des connaissances.

Pour cette raison je tiens à montrer ici un exemple où la combinaison de la parfaite maitrise du végétal et d'une très grande créativité ont transformé de façon spectaculaire l'arbre. Le travail réalisé sur l'arbre peut paraître pour un non initié très spectaculaire. Il est cependant totalement inoffensif et nullement comparable à la rudesse des éléments naturels auxquels l'arbre avait été exposé pendant plusieurs décennies.

On trouve souvent dans des régions montagneuses particulièrement exposées à des extrêmes climatiques, des arbres très intéressants par les parties de Jin et de Shari qu'ils possèdent. Malheureusement souvent ces arbres et tout particulièrement les genévriers développent des troncs longs et fins, couchés sur le sol et complètement disproportionnés par rapport à la taille de l'arbre. La partie inférieure de l'arbre a été protégée par les avalanches et les chutes de pierres. On y retrouve les veines vivantes. Il est bien souvent le seul

BONSAI

Bonsai wird leider immer noch zu oft als ein reines Gärtnerprodukt angesehen. Natürlich werden heute für den Grosshandel in Japan und China kleine Pflänzchen zu Bonsai-ähnlichen Miniaturen 'geschnitten' und zu hunderttausenden exportiert.

Für mich aber ist Bonsai kein Gärtnerprodukt. Ich selbst bin auch nicht Gärtner und auch kein Botaniker. In erster Linie ist Bonsai für mich ein kreatives Schaffen, das Kenntnisse über Perspektive, Tiefenwirkung, Harmonie und Formen erfordert. Selbstverständlich gehört das Wissen über die Pflanze und das Wachstum des Lebewesens genauso dazu. Die ganze kreative Arbeit hat nur einen Sinn, wenn man genau weiss, wie auf das Leben der Pflanze Rücksicht zu nehmen ist. Es nützt aber nichts, wenn ich ein geschulter Gärtner bin aber kein kreatives Talent besitze oder umgekehrt.

Bonsai ist also das Ergebnis kreativer Arbeit an einer lebendigen Pflanze. Nur durch das Multi-Talent und -Kenntnisse werden Erfolge erzielt.

Deshalb möchte ich hier ein Beispiel zeigen, das in Kombination von Pflanzenkenntnissen und Gestaltung zu einer phantastischen, kreativen Veränderung einer Pflanze führt. Die Arbeit an der Pflanze sieht für den Laien eventuell spektakulär aus. für die Pflanze aber ist es ein harmloser Eingriff, der nicht vergleichbar ist mit der 'Brutalität' der Naturgewalten, denen die gleiche Pflanze Jahrzehnte lang ausgesetzt war.

Oft findet man in Bergregionen an klimaextremen Orten, im speziellen Wacholder, die durch eine interessante Jin- und Sharipartie gezeichnet sind. Leider aber einen sehr langen und dünnen Stamm ausgebildet haben. Dieser lange Stamm ist auch oft unverhältnismässig dünn und liegt meistens am Boden. Auf der Unterseite, die vor Lawinen und Steinschlag verschont blieb, befindet sich die Saftbahn. Oft die einzige Lebensader zwischen dem Grünbereich und den Wurzeln.

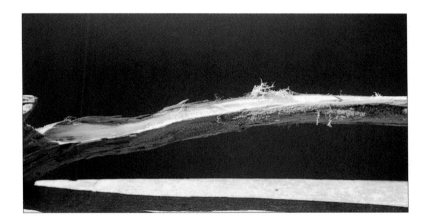

part of the trunk to survive. Only the thin sap-stream on the underside is necessary to keep the plant alive. It is not dangerous to remove the dead wood from the trunk. Removal of the dead wood makes the trunk flexible again. The designer is now able to shorten the trunk by winding it up like a snail. However, precautions must be taken against breaking, interruption or damage to the tender and fragile sap-stream.

Aluminium wire must be attached with raffia along the sap-stream. The raffia is not only a good method of attaching the wire. If correctly applied, it also serves as a second skin, or bark. After the trunk has been shortened through the winding process, the tree can be placed in an appropriate bonsai pot. The remaining design work then consists of wiring and positioning the branches in order to make the design harmonious.

During the first few months after designing, it is important to protect the tree from high evaporation. It should be kept in the shade and not exposed to heat.

dell'albero mantenuto in vita solo dai canali linfatici presenti sul lato posteriore. Se questa parte di legno morto viene completamente eliminata non solo la pianta non soffre, ma il tronco prima rigido, riacquista elasticà e può essere plasmato. Piegandolo a forma di spirale il tronco può essere notevolmente accorciato. Per non danneggiare o interrompere i sottili e delicati canali linfatici si dovranno prendere delle precauzioni. Lungo tutto il tronco vanno inseriti malleabili fili di alluminio, che saranno fissati con la rafla. Essa, se applicata correttamente, non serve solo a fissare i fili, ma anche a sostituire la corteccia mancante, come fosse una seconda pelle.

Dopo la riduzione del tronco attraverso questo procedimento, l'albero può essere posto nel vaso bonsai. Per completare il lavoro la parte verde della pianta va impostata con il fllo e i rami posizionati in modo da formare un piccolo albero armonioso.

Nei primi mesi l'albero va protetto dall'eccessiva evaporazione e tenuto in un luogo fresco e ombroso.

más grueso antes de que las fuerzas naturales despojasen su corteza en la parte superior. La madera a su vez está muerta y decolorada por el sol. El árbol de hecho, no necesita esta parte del troco para poder sobrevivir. Simplemente esa estrecha corriente en la parte inferior,es suficiente para mantener la planta viva. No es perjudicial arrancar la madera seca del tronco. Al retirar esa leña recobramos su flexibilidad. El diseñador entonces, será capaz de recortar el tronco retorciéndole como un caracol. Por supuesto que debemos de tomar precauciones para que no haya ruptura, interrupción o daño cometido a la tierna y frágil corriente de savia.

Alambre de aluminio debe de ser sujeto con rafia a lo largo de la corriente de savia. La rafia no sólo es un buen método de prender el alambre, si es aplicada correctamente servirá como una piel o corteza secundaria. Una vez que el tronco ha sido recortado mediante este proceso, el árbol puede ser plantado en una maceta de bonsai apropiada. El trabajo de su diseño restante, consistirá en el alambrado y reajuste de la posición de las ramas, con la intención de conseguir un resultado más armonioso.

Durante los primeros meses después de haber diseñado, es importante protejer el árbol de demasiada evaporación. Debe de mantenerse en la sombra, y no exponerlo al calor.

lien vivant restant entre les racines et les feuilles. La partie qui fut à l'origine le tronc principal de taille respectable a été écorcé dans la partie supérieure. Le bois est mort maintenant, il a été blanchi par le soleil. Cette partie est inutile à l'arbre. Par contre les parties du cambium dans la partie inférieure sont absolument vitales. Si l'on élimine totalement le bois mort on ne met nullement la vie de l'arbre en danger. Ce tronc qui était auparavent très rigide devient après cette opération flexible, travaillable. Il est maintenant possible au créateur de le raccourcir de façon considérable en l'enroulant sous la forme d'une spirale. Pour éviter que le cambium ne soit blessé, il est très important de prendre toutes les précautions nécessaires. Le long de la partie à plier est disposé du fil d'aluminium, plus adéquat dans ce cas que le cuivre trop dur. Le fil d'aluminium est ensuite fortement fixé par un raffia, lequel sert naturellement à fixer l'aluminium mais surtout, s'il est correctement posé, à former pour l'arbre une deuxième peau ou écorce.

Suite à la réduction de la longueur du tronc par cette technique, l'arbre peut être disposé dans un pot à bonsaï en proportion avec sa taille. Le reste de la création ne consiste plus qu'au ligaturage des branches et leur mise en place de façon à ce que l'ensemble donne l'aspect d'un petit arbre aux formes harmonieuses.

Dans les premiers mois après la mise en place il est très important de protéger l'arbre d'un déssèchement trop rapide et important. Il doit donc être placé à l'ombre à un endroit plutôt frais.

Der ursprünglich viel dickere Hauptstamm ist durch Naturgewalten auf der Oberseite geschält und das Holz ist tot und von der Sonne gebleicht. Diesen Teil des Stammes braucht der Baum eigentlich nicht. für ihn ist nur die relativ dünne Saftbahn auf der Unterseite lebenswichtig. Wenn man nun diesen bereits toten Holzteil vollständig aus dem Stamm entfernt, passiert für den Baum überhaupt nichts Bedrohliches. Der ehemals unbiegsame Stamm wird nun plötzlich biegsam und beweglich. dies ermöglicht es nun dem Gestalter, den viel zu langen Stamm wesentlich zu verkürzten, indem er wie eine Schnecke aufgerollt wird. Damit aber die zarten und filigranen Saftbahnen nicht durch brechen oder reissen unterbrochen werden oder sonstigen Schaden erleiden, ist es wichtig, dass man vorsorgt. Der ganzen Saftbahn entlang werden weiche Aluminium Drähte gelegt, die man mit Raffia gut fixiert. Raffia ist nicht nur zum fixieren des Drahtes, sondern bildet bei korrekter Anbringung eine Art zweite Haut oder Rinde.

Nachdem der Stamm auf diese Weise verkürzt wurde, kann der Baum auch in eine proportional passende Bonsai-Schale gepflanzt werden. Der Rest der Gestaltung besteht dann nur noch aus dem Drahten des Grünbereichs und der Positionierung der einzelnen Äste, damit die ganze Gestaltung einen harmonischen, kleinen Baum ergibt.

In den ersten Monaten nach der Gestaltung ist es wichtig, dass der Baum vor zu starker Verdunstung geschützt wird. Er sollte eher schattiert und nicht zu warm stehen.

▲ **Pinus mugo**
⇕70cm ◁▷100cm

▲ Quercus pubescens
⇕90cm ◁▷180cm

GERMANY

Walter Pall

Walter Pall was born in 1944 and grew up in Austria in the mountains. After studying economics in the USA and in Austria he made a considerable career with prominent companies in the electronic industry and made it to Managing Director. In 1991 he finally settled near Munich as a self-employed management consultant to have more time for his trees.

In 1978 Walter Pall acquired his first bonsai. Already, by the early eighties, he became one of the first serious bonsai designers in Germany and also started to collect trees in nature. Since 1985 his trees have made an impact in exhibitions. He has since then received more than 35 national and international awards.

Walter Pall is especially known for his experience with European trees. He is known for outstanding knowledge about trees and his skills as a tree gardener. As a designer, he works on conifers as well as on deciduous trees with great success. In his garden there are more than 1000 bonsai, most of them collected European trees. In his Bonsai-Atelier one can find, besides the excellent trees, many hundreds of handmade pots, mostly of European origin.

Walter Pall's articles, with the photographs that he takes himself, have appeared in bonsai magazines all over the world. Since 1992 he has held quite popular workshops, demonstrations and slide presentations all over Europe and also in America. He has been a headliner at many national and international conventions.

Since 1993 Walter Pall has been a board member of Bonsaiclub Deutschland, in 1996 he was nominated Director of the worldwide organisation BCI (Bonsai Clubs International) and in 1997 became Vice President of the European Bonsai Association.

Walter Pall è nato nel 1944 ed è cresciuto in una zona montagnosa dell'Austria. Dopo aver studiato economia negli USA ed in Austria si è costruito una brillante carriera con delle società impiegate nell'industria elettronica diventandone Amministratore Delegato. Nel 1991 si è stabilito finalmente a Monaco come consulente amministrativo in proprio, in modo da aver più tempo da dedicare ai suoi alberi.

Nel 1978 Walter Pall acquistò il suo primo albero. Già agli inizi degli anni ottanta era diventato uno dei più quotati bonsaisti in Germania raccogliendo fin dall'ora piante in natura. Dal 1985 i suoi alberi riscossero un grande successo in molte mostre. Da allora ha ricevuto più di 35 premi nazionali ed internazionali.

Walter Pall è rinomato sia per la sua esperienza con alberi Europei che per la sua formidabile conoscenza nell'arte paesaggistica. Ci sono più di 1000 bonsai nel suo giardino, la maggior parte alberi raccolti in Europa. Nel suo Bonsai-Atelier si possono trovare, oltre che a bellissimi bonsai, centinaia di vasi fatti a mano prevalentemente di origine europea.

Gli articoli di Walter Pall, assieme alle foto fatte da lui stesso, sono apparsi su riviste di tutto il mondo. Dal 1992 ha tenuto dimostrazioni di grande successo nonchè presentazioni di diapositive in tutto l'Europa ed anche negli USA. E' stato ospitato in molti congressi nazionali ed internazionali. Dal 1993 Walter Pall è stato socio del consiglio del Bonsaiclub Deutschland e nel 1996 è stato nominato direttore all'organizzazione mondiale BCI (Bonsai Clubs International) e nel 1997 è diventato Vice Presidente dell'Associazione Europeo di Bonsai.

Picea abies
⬍ 99cm
± 100 years / jahre / anni / ans / años
Yamadori 1987
⌷ Derek Aspinall

Carpinus betulus
⇕ 84cm
± 50 years / jahre / anni / ans / años
Yamadori 1986
Bryan Albright

Walter Pall nació en 1944 y se crió en las montañas austriacas. Después de haber estudiado economía en Norte América y Austria adquirio una carrera considerable con companías importantes de industria electrónica hasta llegar a ser director general. En 1991 se estableció finalmente en Munich como asesor administrativo autónomo para poder ocupar más tiempo a sus arboles.

En 1978 Walter Pall adquirio su primer bonsai. Ya entonces al comienzo de la década de los ochenta se convirtió en uno de los primeros diseñadores serios en Alemania y a su vez comenzó a recuperar arboles en la naturaleza. Desde 1985 sus arboles han causado impacto en exhibiciones. Desde entonces ha recibido más de 35 trofeos internacionales.

Walter Pall es especialmente conocido por su experiencia con arboles europeos. Es renombrado por su sabiduria y su destreza para la jardinería arbolista. Como diseñador disfruta trabajando con gran éxito. En su jardín se albergan más de 1000 bonsai, en su gran mayoria arboles cosechados en Europa. En su Bonsai-Atelier, podemos encontrar, además de excelentes árboles, cientos de macetas hechos a mano, en su mayoria Europeos.

Los articulos de Walter Pall, con las fotográfias tomadas por él mismo, han aparecido en revistas del mundo entero. Desde 1992 ha sostenido talleres de gran éxito además de demostraciones. Walter ha aparecido como invitado principal en muchas de las convenciones internacionales. Desde 1993 Walter Pall ha sido miembro de la junta directiva de la Asociación Europea de Bonsai.

Walter Pall est né en 1944. Il grandit en Autriche, à la montagne. Après des études d'économie aux Etats Unis et en Autriche, il fit carrière dans de grandes compagnies d'électronique et en devint Directeur General. En 1991, afin d'avoir plus de temps pour s'occuper de ses arbres, il s'installa en dernier lieu près de Munich pour travailler à son compte en tant qu'expert conseil en administration.

En 1978, Walter Pall acquit son premier bonsaï. Déjà, au début des années quatre vingts, il devint l'un des premiers artistes spécialistes importants de bonsaï en Allemagne et commença à collecter des arbres dans la nature. Depuis 1985, ses arbres ont régulièrement fait forte impression aux expositions. Il a reçu plus de 35 prix nationaux et internationaux.

Walter Pall est surtout reconnu pour son expérience des arbres Européens. Il est connu non seulement pour sa connaissance exceptionnelle des arbres mais aussi pour son savoir faire en tant que jardinier des arbres. En qualité de styliste, il travaille sur les conifères et les arbres à feuilles caduques avec le même succès. Dans son jardin, il y a plus de 1000 bonsaïs, la plupart étant des arbres Européens collectés dans la nature. Dans son «Bonsaï-Atelier», on peut trouver des arbres de qualité mais aussi des centaines de coupes à bonsaï faites à la main, la plupart d'origine Européenne.

Les articles de Walter Pall, illustrés de photos qu'il prend lui-même, sont publiés dans des magazines de bonsaï édités dans le monde entier. Depuis 1992, il organise des ateliers, des démonstrations et des projections de diapositives à travers toute l'Europe et aussi en Amérique. Il a été l'invité d'honneur de beaucoup de conventions nationales et internationales. Depuis 1993, Walter Pall est membre du comité du Bonsaïclub Deutschland. En 1996, il fut élu Directeur de l'organisation mondiale BCI (Bonsaï Clubs International) et en 1997, il devint le Vice President de l'EBA (European Bonsai Association).

Walter Pall er wurde 1944 geboren und ist in Österreich in den Bergen aufgewachsen. Nach dem Studium in den USA und in Österreich hat es der Diplom-Volkswirt bei namhaften Firmen der Elektronikindustrie bis zum Geschäftsführer gebracht. Im Jahr 1991 hat er sich dann in der Nähe von München als Unternehmensberater selbständig gemacht um mehr Zeit für seine Bäume zu haben, die für ihn bis dahin bloß ein Hobby waren.

Im Jahre 1978 erwarb Walter Pall seinen ersten Bonsai. Bereits zu Anfang der 80er Jahre war er einer der ersten ernsthaften Bonsaigestalter Deutschlands und begann Bäume in der Natur zu sammeln. Seit 1985 sind seine Bäume in Ausstellungen aufgefallen. Herr Pall hat seither mehr als 35 nationale und internationale Auszeichnungen erhalten.

Besonders bekannt ist Walter Pall durch seine Erfahrungen mit europäischen Bäumen. Er ist bekannt als ausgezeichneter Baumkenner und Gärtner. Als Gestalter bearbeitet er sowohl Nadelbäume als auch Laubbäume mit großem Erfolg. In seinem Garten stehen mehr als 1000 Bonsais, meistens europäische Findlinge. In seinem Bonsai-Atelier sind neben den hervorragenden Bäumen auch viele hunderte handgemachte Schalen zu finden, die meist aus Europa stammen.

Die Fachartikel von Herrn Pall mit den gelungenen Fotos, die er selbst macht, sind bei Bonsaimagazinen in der ganzen Welt erschienen. Seit 1992 hält er sehr beliebte Workshops, Demos und Diavorträge in ganz Europa und auch in Amerika. Er ist bei vielen nationalen und internationalen Kongressen aufgetreten.

Seit 1993 ist Walter Pall Vorstandsmitglied des Bonsaiclub Deutschland, 1996 wurde er zum Direktor des Weltverbandes Bonsai Club International (BCI) und 1997 zum Vizepräsidenten der European Bonsai Association (EBA) ernannt.

BONSAI ATELIER

WALTER PALL

Sonnenhamer Str. 6
D-82544 Egling-Attenham, Germany
Tel: 0049 (0)8176 455
Fax: 0049 (0)8176 1654

HOW DOES ONE FIND BONSAI?

Not at all! He who walks into nature and seeks bonsai, will not find them. There are, apart from very few exceptions, no trees in nature that one can plant in a pot and call bonsai. What you can find, if anything, is raw-material – more or less interestingly shaped shrubs of which an experienced bonsai designer can make something. Exactly the most confusing and complicated pieces of material are usually the best ones. This is why only an accomplished designer can find really good material. He has to decide, on the spot, about the future design and whether the tree is worthwhile.

Walter Pall

Where should one look for trees? First of all where one has permission to collect or at least a chance to get it. It makes no sense to find the best pieces of material in a natural resort if you may not lift them anyway.

One secret is, to find and not to seek. That means that you are diminishing your chances of success if you go into the forest with the firm intent to find a pine which is most suitable for the formal upright style. Then you will walk by all suitable deciduous trees and will even overlook pines which are good for other styles.

There are people whom you can send to the forest with a large group to find mushrooms and as a rule they find more than the rest of the group together. There are fishermen who always catch more than their buddies together. There are bonsai lovers who find a lot more good trees than a whole club. What do these people have in common? They know a secret, or even a few, that the others don't know. Chances are low that one of them will ever teach you.

So, how can you find such a secret by yourself? Now, everybody will believe that the secret lies in knowing a good place. That's not true! The secret is called pattern recognition. Here is how it works: the bonsai lover walks through the landscape and one day stumbles over a tree that has all

DOVE DI TROVANO I BONSAI?

I bonsai non si trovano! Chiunque che cammina in natura e cerca bonsai non li troverà. Tranne per poche eccezioni, non esistono alberi in natura che si possano piantare in un vaso e chiamare bonsai. Quello che puoi trovare è la materia prima – piante di forme più o meno interessanti e dalle quali un bonsaista con poca esperienza può farci qualcosa. Spesso le piante più complicate costituiscono il materiale migliore. Al momento della raccolta bisogna subito capire quali potenzialità la pianta potrà avere come bonsai.

Dove si trovano gli alberi? Prima di tutto bisogna avere il permesso a raccoglierne o almeno l'opportunità di ottenerlo. Non ha senso trovare i pezzi migliori in natura e non poterli raccogliere comunque.

Un segreto è di trovare e non cercare. Questo vuol dire che avrai meno possibilità di successo se cercherai ostinatamente un tipo di pianta in quel particolare stile, bisogna saper guardare ogni cosa per poi fare la scelta migliore.

Ci sono persone che possono andare nella foresta insieme ad altri per cercare funghi e solitamente trovano più funghi che tutti gli altri messi insieme. Ci sono pescatori che pescano più che tutti i loro amici. Ci sono entusiasti che trovano alberi migliori che un circolo bonsai intero. Che cosa hanno in comune queste persone? Conoscono un segreto o due che gli altri non sanno. Sarà difficilie che uno loro te ne insegni qualcuno.

Ora come si fa trovare un tale segreto da soli? Tutti credono che il segreto sia nel conoscere un buon posto ma non è vero! Il segreto è basato sulla ricognizione del disegno. Ecco come funziona: l'amatore di bonsai cammina nel paesaggio e un giorno trova un'albero che possiede tutti i requisiti per diventare un buon bonsai. Ora ha trovato un buon posto perchè la materia prima – come funghi – cresce in gruppi. Dove ce ne una, l'altra è subito dietro l'angolo.

¿COMO SE ENCUENTRA BONSAI?

¡Imposible! Aquel que vaya a la foresta en busca de un bonsai, no será capaz de encontrarle. No existen, aparte de algunas excepciones, árboles en la naturaleza que podamos recojer, plantar y llamarles bonsai. Lo que sí que podemos hallar es lo que se conoce como material crudo (bruto) arbustos con formas más o menos interesantes, de los cuales un diseñador de bonsai experto puede conseguir algo. Precisamente los materiales más complejos y confusos son normalmente los más interesantes. Por esta razón sólo el diseñador más hábil logra hallar material realmente bueno. Tiene que decidir en ese preciso instante sobre el futuro diseño y si el árbol merece la pena.

¿Dónde se deben de buscar los árboles? Primeramente en las áreas donde esté permitido o donde quepa la posibilidad de obtener permiso. No tiene sentido el buscar en un lugar donde después de un hallazgo no se nos permita la colecta. Uno de los secretos es el encontrar y no el buscar. Esto quiere decir que estamos disminuyendo nuestras oportunidades al adentrarse en la foresta con el mero hecho de encontrar un pino idóneo para el estilo formal recio. De esta manera fácilmente se puede pasar al lado de árboles de hoja caduca e incluso despreciaremos pinos que sean adecuados para otros estilos.

Existen personas que podemos enviar en grupo para buscar setas, y generalmente encuentran ellos solos más hongos que el resto del grupo junto. Hay pescadores que pescan más que todos sus colegas. Hay apasionados del bonsai que encuentran más y mejores árboles que todo un club junto. ¿Qué tiene esta gente en común? Saben un secreto, o incluso varios, que los otros no conocen. Oportunidades hay pocas por lo tanto una, jamás te enseñará. ¿Entonces como hallamos este secreto nosotros mismos? Ahora, todo el mundo creerá que el secreto se halla en el saber de un lugar ideal. ¡Esto, no es verdad! El secreto se llama, "patrón de

COMMENT TROUVER UN BONSAI?

Ce n'est pas si facile que ça! Celui qui va chercher un bonsaï dans la nature ne le trouvera pas. A part quelques exceptions, un arbre trouvé dans la nature et planté dans un pot ne mérite pas le nom de bonsaï. Ce qu'on peut trouver, c'est la matière première pour créer un bonsaï – des arbustes aux formes intéressantes, avec lesquelles un artiste en bonsaï expérimenté peut travailler. Les arbustes les plus confus et compliqués ont le plus de potentiel. Pour cette raison, seul un styliste expérimenté peut y trouver la bonne matière première. Il doit décider, sur place, du futur style de l'arbre et choisir s'il vaut la peine d'être déterré.

Où doit-on aller pour chercher ces arbres? En premier lieu là où on la permission de collecter ou au moins la chance de l'obtenir. Ça ne servirait à rien de trouver la matière brute idéale si l'on ne peut déterrer d'arbre à cet endroit.

Le secret: trouver sans chercher. On réduit ses chances de succès si l'on entre dans une forêt avec l'intention de trouver un pin que l'on veut styliser en forme rigoureusement verticale. On risque alors de passer à côté de tous les arbres à feuilles caduques qui auraient été adéquats et de ne même pas remarquer les pins qui auraient convenus à d'autres styles.

Certaines personnes peuvent être envoyées dans la forêt pour chercher des champignons avec tout un groupe de gens, et elles en trouveront toujours plus que les autres. Il y a aussi ces pêcheurs qui attrapent toujours plus de poissons que les autres. Et enfin, il y a ces amoureux de bonsaï qui trouvent toujours de plus beaux arbres que tous les membres de leur club réunis. Qu'est-ce qu'ils ont tous en commun? Ils connaissent un secret, ou plusieurs, que les autres ne connaissent pas. Toutefois, il y a peu de chances qu'ils le partagent avec vous!

Alors, comment découvrir ce secret par vous-même? Tout le monde va croire que ce secret consiste en la connaissance d'un

WIE FINDET MAN BONSAIS?

Überhaupt nicht! Wer in die Natur geht und Bonsais sucht, der wird keine finden. Es gibt, bis auf ganz wenige Ausnahmen, in der Natur keine Bäume, die man bloß in eine Schale setzen und dann Bonsai nennen kann. Man findet höchstens gutes Rohmaterial, nämlich mehr oder weniger interessant geformte Gestrüppe, aus denen der erfahrene Bonsaigestalter etwas machen kann. Gerade die besonders verwirrenden, komplizierten Rohlinge sind meistens die besten. Deshalb kann nur ein langjähriger Gestalter wirklich gutes Material finden, weil er ja bereits vor Ort die Grundform sehen muß um zu entscheiden, ob der Rohling brauchbar ist.

Wo kann man generell suchen? Erstens dort, wo man auch eine Genehmigung zum Sammeln hat, oder wenigstens Aussicht auf eine besteht. Es macht keine Sinn, in Naturschutzgebieten die besten Rohlinge ausfindig zu machen, wenn man ohnehin keinen ausgraben darf.

Die Kunst ist es, zu finden und nicht zu suchen. D.h., es hat wenig Aussicht auf Erfolg, in die Natur zu gehen mit dem festen Vorsatz, einen Kiefernrohling zu finden, der sich ideal für die Streng Aufrechte Form eignet und dann an allen wirklich brauchbaren Laubbäumen vorüberzugehen und selbst Kiefern zu übersehen, die sich für andere Stilarten hervorragend eignen.

Es gibt Menschen, die kann man mit einer Gruppe in den Wald schicken um Pilze zu sammeln und sie finden regelmäßig mehr als der Rest der Gruppe zusammen. Es gibt Fischer, die fangen immer mehr als ihre Kollegen zusammen. Es gibt Bonsaifreunde, die finden wesentlich mehr gute Bäume als ganze Arbeitskreise zusammen. Was haben diese Menschen gemeinsam? Sie kennen ein Geheimnis oder gar mehrere, das die anderen nicht kennen. Die Chancen, daß man von so einem in die Lehre genommen wird, stehen schlecht.

Wie kann man also selbst so ein

A very old larch with enormous potential is being cut back on the spot
Si sta potando sul posto un molto vecchio larice che ha potenziale enorme
Un alerce antigüo con un gran potencial esta siendo recortado en el lugar mismo
Un très vieux larix avec d'énormes possibilités d'être taillé sur place
Eine sehr alte Lärche wird am Fundort Zurechtgeschnitten

This Pinus mugo sat on the rock for several hundred years. It will have a very good chance of survival after collection

Questo Pinus mugo rimarse sulla roccia per centinaia di anni. Avrà una molto buona probabilità di sopravvivenza dopo esser stato scavato

Este P{inus mugo ha estado asentado en esta roca durante varios cientos de años. La probabilidad de supervivencia, una vez cosechado, será muy alta

Ce pinus mugo resta sur le rocher pendant plusiers centaines d'années. Il avra de très bonnes chances de survivre après avoir été déterrè

Diese Pinus mugo sitz seit mehreren hundert Jahren auf dem Felsen, Sie hat eine sehr hohe Überlebenschance nach dem Sammeln

This gigantic Picea abies was prepared by cattle on an alpine pasture over a few centuries

Quest gigantesco Picea abies fu praparato dal bestiame su un pascolo alpino nel corso di parecchi secoli

Esta Picea abies gigante, ha sido previamente preparada por el ganado en los pastos alpinos, durante varios siglos

Ce gigantesque Picea abies fut préparé par les bovins sur une pâture alpine au cours de quelque siècles

Diese gigantische Fichte wurde auf einer Alm von Kühen über mehrere Jahrhunderte vorbereitet

the requirements to become a good bonsai. Now he has found a good place, because raw material, like mushrooms comes in groups - where there is one, the next one is just around the corner.

You have to realise, that the secret is not to find a good place, but to find one again and again, also in areas where you have never been before. The bonsai lover goes on looking for good trees and by accident finds another one. Then the successful one starts to query: what have the two places in common, why is it that the trees are so nice and small? If, for example, in both places there was a deer feeding area where, in winter, the animals grazed upon the trees and kept them small, then he has a pattern! With this pattern he will have a great chance to find something wherever there are deer feeding places.

The very successful collector finds out later that there are a whole lot of these patterns that have the scent of good material. He assembles more and more knowledge about trees, speaks to them, understands them better all the time and finds more and better ones.

A good time to look for trees is when you cannot collect them because it is the wrong time of the year. Then you are not tempted to take the very first one. Since there are only a few weeks in spring and possibly in autumn when one should lift a tree with some hope of success, there is a long period when you can try to find them.

Bisogna capire che il segreto non è nel trovare un buon posto ma di trovarne uno dopo l'altro, anche in zone dove non sei mai stato. L'amatore di bonsai continua a cercare buoni alberi e per caso ne trova un'altro. Poi si chiede che cos'hanno in comune i due posti e perchè gli alberi sono così piccoli e belli. Se per esempio in tutti e due i posti c'erano dei cervi che, durante inverno, pascolavano sugli alberi tenendoli piccoli, allora c'è un collegamento! Con questo collegamento il ricercatore avrà più probabilità di trovare qualcosa dovunque pascolano i cervi.

Un raccoglitore di successo scopre una buona zona dove raccogliere solo se è abile nell'interpretare tutti questi segni. Raccoglie sempre più conoscenza degli alberi, gli parla, gli capisce sempre meglio e trova esemplari sempre di più belli.

Un buon periodo per cercare gli alberi è quando non li puoi raccogliere perchè non è stagione. Allora non sei tentato di prelevare il primo che trovi. Visto che ci sono poche settimane in primavera e possibilmente in autunno quando si possono raccogliere alberi con una certa probabilità di successo, esiste un lungo periodo nel quale li si può cercare.

reconocimiento". Y funciona de esta manera: El aficionado de bonsai camina a través del bosque y un día tropieza con un árbol que guarda todos los atributos para convertirse en un buen bonsai. Ahora esta persona ha encontrado un lugar propicio, por que el material bruto viene como las setas, en grupos, donde hay uno, el próximo estará a la vuelta de la esquina.

Debemos de darnos cuenta que el secreto no es el encontrar un buen lugar si no el hallar uno, una vez y otra también en áreas donde no hemos estado anteriormente.

El amante de bonsai persevera en la búsqueda de buenos árboles y por casualidad encuentra otro. Luego el afortunado se pregunta a sí mismo ¿Qué tienen estos dos lugares en común? ¿Por qué razón son los árboles tan bonitos y pequeños? Si por ejemplo las dos son zonas de pasto para ciervos, donde en invierno los animales pastan los arboles manteniéndoles de un tamano pequeño, ¡he ahí un patrón! Con esta pauta tendrá mayor oportunidad de un hallazgo en las áreas donde se dé el pasto de ciervos.

El coleccionista con gran éxito, comprende que hay una serie de patrones y que poseen el olfato del buen material. El agrupa más y más conocimiento sobre árboles, habla con ellos, les entiende mejor cuanto más tiempo transcurre, y los encuentra cada vez mejores.

Un búen momento para encontrar arboles, es cuando es el tiempo erróneo del año para buscar. Entonces uno no está tentado en recojer el primero que vea. Ya que sólo hay unas pocas semanas en primavera y posiblemente en otoño donde podemos trasplantar un árbol con esperanza de éxito, existe un periodo largo, donde podemos tratar de encontrarles.

bon endroit pour collecter les arbres. Mais ce n'est pas vrai! Le secret consiste à reconnaitre un modèle d'identification. Voilà comment ça marche: l'amoureux de bonsaï se promène à travers la campagne et un jour, il tombe sur un arbre qui a tout ce qui faut pour devenir un arbre de qualité. Dès lors, il a trouvé un bon endroit, parceque comme les champignons poussent en groupe, la matière première apparait regroupée – une découverte en assure une autre toute proche.

Il faut savoir que le secret n'est pas de trouver un bon endroit mais de trouver de bons endroits régulièrement, même dans des coins où l'on n'a jamais mis les pieds. L'amoureux de bonsaï est toujours en train de chercher de beaux arbres, et par hasard, il en trouve de nouveaux. Alors, celui qui réussit à trouver se demande ce que ces deux endroits ont en commun? Pourquoi les arbres y sont-ils si beaux et si petits? Si par exemple dans les deux endroits les cerfs se nourrissent en hiver en broutant les arbres, ce qui les conserve tout petits, il a trouvé son modèle. Aves ce modèle, il a de grandes chances de trouver quelque chose d'intéressant partout où les cerfs se nourrissent.

Le collecteur qui a souvent du succès apprend vite qu'il y a un grand nombre de modèles qui mettent sur la piste d'excellente matière première. Il accumule de plus en plus de connaissances sur les arbres, leur parle, les comprend toujours mieux et en trouve de plus en plus et de meilleure qualité.

La meilleure période pour aller chercher des arbres est la mauvaise saison: quand on ne peut pas les déterrer. Alors, on n'est pas tenté de collecter le premier arbre venu. Il n'y a que quelques semaines au printemps et en automne pour déterrer un arbre avec une chance de succès mais une longue période pour chercher.

Geheimnis entdecken? Nun wird jeder glauben, daß das Geheimnis in der Kenntnis einer guten Fundstelle liegt. Das stimmt nicht, das Geheimnis besteht in der Mustererkennung. Das funktioniert so: Der Bonsaifreund wandert durch die Landschaft und stolpert irgendwann über einen Baum, der alle Voraussetzungen für einen guten Bonsai hat. Dann hat er erst einmal einen guten Platz gefunden, denn Bonsairohlinge kommen, wie Pilze, in Gruppen vor - wo einer steht, da steht ein zweiter um die Ecke.

Man muß wissen, daß es gar nicht darum geht, einen besonders guten Platz zu wissen, sondern darum, einen solchen immer wieder zu finden, auch in Gegenden, wo man noch nie war. Wenn er woanders weitersucht und wieder durch Zufall auf einen guten Rohling stößt, dann beginnt der Erfolgreiche zu kombinieren: Was haben die beiden Plätze gemeinsam, was bewirkt an beiden Fundorten, daß die Bäume so schön klein bleiben. Wenn es z.B. so ist, daß an beiden Stellen durch die Nähe einer Wildfütterung im Winter die Hirsche den kleinen Buchen die Triebe abnagen, dann hat er ein Muster. Mit diesem Muster wird er dann überall, wo es Wildfütterungen gibt, eine große Chance auf Erfolg haben.

Der sehr Erfolgreiche kommt dann später zur Erkenntnis, daß es eine ganze Reihe von solchen Mustern gibt, die zielführend sind. Er eignet sich immer mehr Wissen über die Bäume an, hält Zwiesprache mit ihnen, versteht sie immer besser und findet immer mehr und geeignetere.

Es ist eine gute Zeit Bäume zu suchen, wenn man sie wegen der Jahreszeit gar nicht ausgraben kann. Dann kommt man nämlich gar nicht erst in Versuchung und nimmt auch nicht gleich den ersten besten. Nachdem man nur kurze Zeit im Herbst und einige Wochen im Frühjahr mit Aussicht auf Erfolg einen Baum ausgraben sollte, hat man somit sehr viel Zeit dazwischen zur Auswahl.

Pinus mugo montana
↕ 74cm
± 100 years / jahre / anni / ans / años
Yamadori 1984
Peter Krebs

▲ **Juniperus communis repanda**
⬍ 82cm ◁▷ 82cm
± 200 years / jahre / anni / ans / años
Yamadori 1994
▭ Derek Aspinall

FRANCE

Patrick Richert

Since childhood Patrick Richert has had a passion for all things Japanese. An intense practitioner of martial arts, he loves nature, and at the age of nine wanted to become a forest ranger. Early adult life led to a career as radio personality, giving him a facility for public speaking.

In 1984, he received a Bonsai tree as a gift. It quickly faded and died, but no-one was able to explain why. He then devoured all the books on Bonsai he could find. To put a bit of practical training behind the theory, he worked free of charge for several importers. In 1986, the director of the garden centre Le Point Vert gave him the chance to use his training by opening a Bonsai department. In 1991 he founded Bonsai Service. A name which expresses his desire to be of service to the world of bonsai, with a bonsai care centre and workshop.

'Bonsai is a living art; to be professional, you have to master the cultivation and aesthetic' A self-starter, he worked hard to learn the basics of horticulture. During his travels in Asia, and while working with some of the biggest names in Bonsai, he acquired the techniques and adapted them to our climate.

To him, nothing is final; he is constantly questioning the status quo in the search for better results. His motto is, 'advance one step at a time; learn and transmit the principles of Bonsai'. Today member of a guild of bonsai professionals and a judge in the Bonsai Federation of France, he hopes to see the level of quality in today's bonsai rise. He organises numerous bonsai classes for all levels, participates in conferences and is never stingy with advice. Today, after having been a precursor in the art of Bonsai, he is taking on two new challenges; to introduce Japanese Koi carp, and Japanese gardens to the French public.

Da quando era bambino, Patrick Richert ha avuto una passione per tutto ciò che era giapponese. Pratica le arti marziali intensamente e ama la natura. Quando aveva nove anni voleva diventare forestale. Da giovane a intrapreso la carriera di speaker radiofonico, acrui sendo la facilità di parlare in pubblico. Nel 1984 gli è stato regalato un albero bonsai, il quale mori velocemente. Nessuno riusci a spiegarsi il perchè. Patrick ha poi divorato tutti i libri di bonsai disponibili e per mettere in pratica gli insegnamenti ricevuti ha lavorato gratis per alcuni importatori. Nel 1986 il direttore del centro di giardinaggio Le Point Vert gli ha dato la possibilità di dimostrare la sua abilità mediante l'apertura di un reparto di bonsai. Nel 1991 ha fondato la Bonsai Service, un nome che esprime il suo desiderio di offrire servizi al mondo bonsai, con un centro di cura bonsai e laboratorio per dimostrazioni.

Bonsai è un'arte vivente, per essere un vero professionista devi conoscere a fondo la coltivazione e l'estetica. Avendo imparato da solo, ha lavorato intensamente per imparare le basi dell'orticoltura. Durante i suoi viaggi in Asia e mentre collaborava con alcuni dei nomi più prestigiosi del mondo, ha acquisito delle tecniche che ha succesivamente adattato al nostro clima.

Per lui, niente finisce e interroga constantamente lo status quo alla ricerca di risultati migliori. Il suo motto è avanzare ad un passo alla volta: impara a trasmettere i principi del bonsai. Attualmente è socio dell'associazione per bonsaisti professionisti e giudice nella Federazione Bonsai di Francia. Patrick spera di vedere alzarsi il livello di qualità dei bonsai odierni. Organizza molte lezioni di bonsai a tutti i livelli, partecipa a conferenze ed è sempre disponibile a dare consigli a tutti. Ora, dopo essere stato un precursore nell'arte del bonsai, ha intrapreso due nuove sfide: far conoscere le famose carpe e i giardini giapponesi al pubblico francese.

Desde su infancia, Patrick Richert, se ha apasionado por todo lo relacionado con Japón. Un gran aficionado a las artes marciales, amante de la naturaleza ya a los nueve años quería ser guardia forestal. En sus comienzos profesionales se convirtió en una personalidad de radio, dotándole esto de una gran facilidad de palabra con el público.

En 1984, recibió un árbol Bonsai como regalo. Pero rápidamente se debilitó y murió, y nadie le pudo explicar por qué. Más tarde comenzó a devorar todos los libros referentes a bonsai que caian en sus manos. Para poder poner una base práctica tras toda esta teoría, trabajó voluntariamente para diversos importadores. En 1986, el director del centro botánico "Le point vert" Le otorgó la oportunidad de poner en práctica todo su aprendizaje, mediante la apertura de un departamento de Bonsai. En 1991 fué fundador del 'Bonsai Service'. El nombre mismo expresa su deseo de servir al mundo del bonsai con un centro del cuidado y talleres.

Bonsai es un arte vivo, "Para poder ser profesional debemos de dominar el cultivo y la estética". Como autodidacta, Patrick tuvo que trabajar muy duramente para poder aprender las bases de horticultura. Durante sus viajes a Asia, y mientras trabajaba con algunos de los nombres más importantes de bonsai, adquirio las técnicas necesarias para adaptarlas consecuentemente a nuestro clima.

Para el, nada es final, Patrick se cuestiona constantemente el status-quo en la búsqueda de mejores resultados. Su lema es "avanzar paso a paso" aprender a transmitir los principios de bonsai. Hoy miembro de un gremio de profesionales de bonsai y juez de la Federación de Bonsai Francesa, espera ver un ascenso en el nivel de calidad del bonsai actual. Organiza numerosas clases de bonsai para todos los niveles, participa en conferencias y nunca es tacaño a la hora de dar consejos. Hoy en día, después de haber sido precursor en el arte de Bonsai, tiene dos nuevos retos; introducir la carpa Koi y jardines japoneses para el publico frances.

Depuis son plus jeune âge Patrick Richert est passionné par le Japon. Il pratique intensément les arts martiaux et est très souvent au contact de la nature, à l'âge de 9 ans il désire devenir garde forestier. La vie en décide autrement et le mène dans une carrière d'animateur radio. Ce qui lui permet d'acquérir une facilité d'élocution en public.

En 1984 il reçoit un bonsaï en cadeau, celui-ci meurt rapidement et personne ne peut lui dire pourquoi. C'est à ce moment qu'il décide d'en savoir plus. Il dévore tous les livres qu'il trouve. Pour mettre un peu de pratique sur la théorie, il va travailler gratuitement, chez quelques importateurs. Puis il quitte la communication pour devenir salarié du bonsaï en 1986. Le dirigeant de l'enterprise Le Point Vert lui donne sa chance en ouvrant un département bonsaï. C'est au mois de mai 1991 qu'il décide de créer sa propre entreprise: bonsaï Service – un nom qui reésume sa vocation, être au service du bonsaï.

«Le bonsaï est un art vivant, pour être un bon professionnel, il faut maîtriser la culture et l'ésthétisme.» Etant autodidacte il travail dur pour apprendre les bases de l'horticulture. Durant ses déplacements en Asie, et en côtoyant les plus grands noms du bonsaï il acquiert les techniques et les adaptes à notre climat. Pour lui rien n'est définitif, il ne cesse de remettre en cause les certitudes pour obtenir de meilleurs résultats.

Sa devise: «avancer pas à pas, comprendre et transmettre le principe du bonsaï». Il est aujourd'hui, membre de la guilde des professionnels (une association qui garantit pour la qualité). Il organise de nombreuses journées de formation, participe aux conférences et n'est jamais avare de conseils. Son rêve, voir le bonsaï être reconnu comme une véritable œuvre d'art et non comme un vulgaire objet de décoration. Après avoir été un précurseur dans l'art du bonsaï il tente aujourd'hui deux nouveaux paris, faire découvrir les carpes Koï et les jardins Japonais en France.

Seit seiner Kindheit hat Patrick Richert eine Passion für alle japanischen Dinge. Er ist ein starker Anhänger kriegerischer Künste, liebt die Natur und wollte mit neun Jahren Förster werden. Das junge Erwachsenendasein führte ihn zu einer Karriere beim Rundfunk, die ihm die Vorteile öffentlicher Reden bescherten.

1984 erhielt er einen Bonsai als Geschenk. Schnell wurde der Bonsai schwach und starb und niemand konnte erklären, warum. Von da an verschlang er alle Bonsaibücher, die er finden konnte. Um die Theorie mit etwas praktischem Training zu untermauern, arbeitete er kostenlos für verschiedene Importeure. 1986 gab ihm der Kirecktor des Gartenzentrums 'Le Point Vert' die Möglichkeit seine Schulung zu nutzen und eröffnete eine Bonsaiabteilung. 1991 gründete er den 'Bonsai Service'. Ein Name, der seinen Wunsch ausfrückt, der Bonsaiwelt zu Diensten zu sein. Angeschlossen war ein Bonsai-Pflegezentrum und ein Workshop.

Für ihn ist nichts endgültig, er zweifelt dauernd den Status quo auf der Suche nach besseren Ergebnissen an. Sein Motto ist: 'Mache einen Schritt nach dem anderen, lerne und übertrage die Prinzipien von Bonsai'. Heute ist er Mitglied einer Gilde von Bonsaiprofis und Preisrichter für den französischen Verband. Er hofft, daß das qualitätsniveau der heutigen Bonsai steigt. Er organisiert unzählige Bonsaischulungen für Anfänger und Fortgeschrittene, nimmt an Konferenzen teil und geizt nicht mit Ratschlägen. Heutzutage, nachdem er Vorbote für die Bonsaikunst war, hat er zwei neue Herausforderungen: japanische Kois und japanische Gärten in der französischen Öffentlichkeit einzuführen.

PATRICK RICHERT

Le Point Vert, 2 route de Didenheim, 68720 Hochstatt, France
Tel: 0033 (0)3 89 06 27 66

Patrick Richert

BONSAI

Bonsai is an art from apart, living and increasing, constantly evolving. This art can only exist if the artist masters the basics of horticulture (keeping the tree in good health and understanding the growth process), and he applies basic aesthetic rules (proportion, perspective, emotional character) to his work. The viewer, in discovering the miniature tree, will be drawn in if all these elements are united. One quickly forgets the small size, and recaptures the emotions of being under a tree surrounded by nature's intoxicating force.

To me, bonsai is a means of communication, a reflection of the personality, a way of expressing the deepest feelings within us. It is, above all, a concept. One must find and bring to being the bonsai in oneself, for it is in this way a form of communication with nature, a true reciprocal action; the tree acts upon the man just as the man acts upon the tree. One word sums up all these sensations – harmony.

Some say 'Only trees found in nature are true bonsai'. This way of thinking rejects the very essence of the art. The end is one thing, the means another. However, in no case do I believe that an Alsatian cow munching on the tender spring leaves of a plant would have more merit than a Japanese gardener working with passion and experience. An open mind and an ongoing search for perfection don't allow restrictive thought. To go forward, one must experiment with all the techniques. Staring from seed is an excellent way to perfect the classic forms, but it takes many years to obtain results. Meanwhile we can learn with nursery plants or trees from Japan. Since the latter are between 10 and 200 years of age, we may avoid waiting a similar amount of time to enjoy the pleasures of trying other techniques (in the event that we don't live quite that long!). Through our progress, we can make more and more detailed modifications to our trees, to improve their aesthetics. Bonsai is

BONSAI

Bonsai è una forma d'arte separata, vivendo e crescendo, evolvendo costantemente. Quest'arte può esistere soltanto se l'artista conosce a fondo le basi dell'orticoltura (tenendo l'albero in buona salute e capendo il processo di crescita) e se applica delle regole di base dell'estetica (proporzione, prospettiva, capacità espressiva) al suo lavoro.

Lo spettatore, scoprendo l'albero in miniatura, verrà convolto se tutti questi elementi sono uniti. Così si dimentica facilmente la dimensione piccola e si ritrovano le emozioni di sentirsi sotto un'albero circondato dalla forza della natura.

Per me bonsai è un veicolo di comunicazione, il riflesso della personalità, un modo per esprimere i sentimenti più profondi dentro noi stessi perchè in questo modo diventa una forma di comunicazione con la natura, una vera azione reciproca: l'albero influisce sull'uomo come l'uomo influisce sill'albero. Una parola raggruppa tutti questi sentimenti – l'armonia.

Certi dicono "soltanto gli alberi trovati in natura sono veri bonsai", questo modo di pensare respinge l'esatta essenza dell'arte. Il fine è una cosa, il mezzo per farlo è un altro. Comunque, non credo che una mucca Alsaziana pascolando su delle foglie tenera primaverile abbia più merito che un giardiniere giapponese lavorando con passione ed esperienza. Una mente aperta e una ricerca continua per la perfezione non permette pensieri limitati. Per avanzare bisogna sperimentare tutti le tecniche.

Iniziare dal seme è un metodo eccezionale per perfezionare le forme classiche. ma ci vogliono molti anni per ottenere dei risultati, mentre possiamo imparare utilizzando piante da vivaio o alberi dal Giappone. Dato che quest'ultimi hanno spesso dai 10 ai 200 anni, possiamo dunque evitare di aspettare altrettanti anni per godere del piacere di provare altre tecniche (visto che non viviamo così a lungo). Attraverso il nostro progresso possiamo

BONSAI

Bonsai es una forma artística aparte. Viva crecedera y evolucionando constantemente. Este arte solamente puede existir si el artista domina las bases horticulturales (el mantener el árbol con una salud óptima y entender el proceso de su crecimiento), y aplicar las bases de reglas estéticas (proporción, perspectiva, y carácter emocional) a su trabajo. El espectador, al descubrir este árbol miniaturizado, se sentirá atraido como si todos estos elementos estuviesen alli unidos. Uno mismo olvida fácilmente el tamaño diminuto, y recaptura, las emociones de hallarse bajo un árbol, rodeado de la fuerza intoxicante de la naturaleza.

Para mí, bonsai es un medio de comunicación, un reflejo de la personalidad, una forma de expresar las sentimientos más profundos escondidos dentro de cada individuo. Es sobre todo, un concepto. Debemos de encontrar y llevar el bonsai dentro de uno mismo, ya que de esta manera, se trama una forma de comunicación con la naturaleza, una acción verdaderamente recíproca; el árbol actúa sobre el hombre tal como el hombre actúa sobre el árbol. Hay una palabra que sintetiza todas estas emociones - 'armonía'.

Algunas personas dicen "Solamente los árboles, encontrados en la naturaleza pueden ser denominados como bonsai". Esta forma de pensar rechaza la esencia misma del arte. El producto final es una cosa, sus procedimientos otra. De todas las maneras, no creo en ningún caso, que una vaca alsaciana, que pasta de las tiernas hojas de una planta, pueda tener mas mérito que un jardinero japonés, que trabaja con pasión y experiencia. Una mente abierta y una constante búsqueda por la perfección no nos permite una forma de pensar restringida. Para poder seguir adelante, debemos experimentar con todas las técnicas. Comenzar con semillas es una forma excelente para perfeccionar las formas clásicas, pero se debe de invertir mucho tiempo para obtener resultados.

LE BONSAI

Le bonsaï est une œuvre d'art à part entière, vivante de surcroît, donc en constante évolution. Cet art ne peut exister que si l'artiste maîtrise les bases de l'horticulture (maintenir l'arbre en bonne santé et comprendre son processus de croissance) et s'il applique à son travail des règles esthétiques de base (les proportions, la perspective, et le caractère émotionnel). Le spectateur qui découvre un arbre miniature sera interpellé, si tous ces éléments sont réunis. Alors très vite on oublie sa petite taille et l'on retrouve l'émotion d'être sous un arbre dans la nature dont la force nous enivre.

Le bonsaï est pour moi un moyen de communication, un reflet de la personnalité, une manière d'exprimer les sentiments les plus profonds qui nous animent. C'est avant tout un concept, il faut réaliser l'arbre qui est en nous et le matérialiser. C'est par ce biais une manière de communiquer avec la nature, une véritable action de réciprocité: l'arbre agit sur l'homme en même temps que l'homme agit sur l'arbre. Ainsi nous comprendrons mieux les forces de l'univers et nous grandirons en même temps que l'arbre. Un seul mot résume toutes ses sensations: l'Harmonie.

Certain pensent: «Seuls les arbres trouvés dans la nature sont les vrais bonsaï» de cette manière ils en rejettent l'essence même. Le résultat est une chose, la façon d'y arriver en est une autre. En aucune une vache Alsacienne en broutant les feuilles tendres du printemps aurait plus de mérite qu'un pépiniériste Japonais animé de passion et d'expérience.

L'ouverture d'esprit, et une constante recherche de la perfection ne m'autorisent ces pensées restrictives. Pour aller de l'avant il faut expérimenter toutes les techniques. Le semis est une excellente manière pour se perfectionner aux formes classiques, mais il faut de nombreuses années avant d'obtenir les résultats. Pendant ce temps on peut apprendre avec des arbres de pépinière ou des arbres d'origine

BONSAI

Bonsai ist eine Kunstform - besonders, lebendig, wachsend, sich dauernd entwicklend. Diese Kunst kann nur bestehen, wenn der Künstler die Grundlagen der Hortikultur beherrscht (den Baum in guter Gesundheit halten und die Wachstumsprozesse verstehen) und wenn er die ästhetischen Grundregeln bei seinen Werken anwendet (Proportionen, Perspektive, emotioneller Charakter).

Der Betrachter, der den Miniaturbaum entdeckt, wird sich zu ihm hingezogen fühlen, wenn alle diese Elemente vereint sind. Man vergißt schnell die kleine Größe und erlangt wieder die Emotionen als stünde man unter einem Baum, umgeben von den berauschenden Kräften der Natur.

Für mich ist Bonsai ein Kommunikationsmittel, eine Zurückstrahlung der Persönlichkeit, ein Weg unsere tiefsten Gefühle auszudrücken. Darüberhinaus ist es ein Konzept. Man muß den Geist von Bonsai in sich finden und verwirklichen, denn dann ist es eine der Kommunikation mit der Natur, der Baum wirkt auf den Menschen ein, so wie der Mensch auf den Baum einwirkt. Ein Wort faßt alle diese Empfindungen zusammen - Harmonie.

Einige sagen 'Nur in der Natur gefundene Bäume sind wahre Bonsai'. Diese Art zu denken, lehnt den wahren Geist dieser Kunst ab. Der Zweck ist ein Weg, die Mittel ein anderer. Ich glaube jedoch auf keinen Fall, daß eine elsässische Kuh, die an den zarten Frühlingsblättern einer Pflanze herumkaut mehr Vorzuge hat als ein japanischer Gärtner, der mit Leidenschaft und erfahrung arbeitet. Ein offener Verstand und eine fortwährende Suche nach Perfektion erlauben keine einschränkenden Gedanken.

Wenn man weiterkommen will, muß man alle Techniken ausprobieren. Die Aufzucht aus Samen ist ein ausgezeichneter Weg, die klassischen Formen zu perfektionieren, aber es dauert viele Jahre, bis man Ergebnis erzielt. In der Zwischenzeit können wir an Baumschulpflanzen oder

4

5

an evolving art. Yamadori, the making tree from nature, is an approach that enables us to work on a tree that has been forged by the nature.

In Conclusion, only the pleasure of working on a tree that will make me grow is worth experiencing.

This Chinese Juniper no longer resembles a Bonsai (photo 1). After having assured myself of its good health, I tried to restructure it completely, this being the first step (Photo 2) Once the growth had restarted, it was repotted and repositioned.(photo 3) The rest is left to time, and in six months the metamorphosis will continue.

This five needle Pine (x Kokonge) is a good example. (photo 4) If it is not pruned regularly, it becomes too tufted, loses its character, as well as all internal ramification, and finally resembles more a brush than a bonsai. It's early July, the pine is in fine form and has vigorous roots. This pruning to thin is the first phase in the restructuring of the tree. We have taken off all of the young shoots back to the two-year-old growth. During the summer, sunlight will penetrate into the interior branches and make new buds appear. This will permit us to make a second branch selection before the wiring in November or December. (photo 5)

effettuare sempre più modifiche ai nostri alberi creati dalla natura ci permette di lavorare con un albero formato da eventi atmosferici naturali.

Infine vale la plena di vivere anche solo per il piacere di lavorare un albero e di crescere insieme a lui.

Questo ginepro cinese non sembrava più un bonsai (foto 1). Dopo essermi assicurato della sua salute ho cercato di ristrutturarlo completamente, questo è il primo passo (foto 2). Quando ha iniziato a crescere, fu rinvasato e riposizionato (foto 3). Tutto il resto rimane nelle mani del tempo e tra sei mesi la metamorfosi continuerà.

Questo pino a cinque aghi (x Kokonge) è un buon esempio (foto 4) se non viene potato regolarmente diventa troppo folto, perde sia carattere che ramificazione interna e assomiglia alla fine ad una spazzola invece di un bonsai. Sono i primi di Luglio ed il pino è in buonissima salute e ha delle radici vigorosi. La prima fase nella ristrutturazione dell'albero è di potarlo in modo di rendere l'albero più snello. Abbiamo rimosso tutti i nuovi germogli fino alla parte della crescita di due anni. Durante l'estate il sole penetrerà tra i rami e spunteranno nuovi germogli. Ciò ci permetterà di fare una seconda selezione dei rami prima della filatura in Novembre o Dicembre (foto 5).

Mientras que podemos aprender con plantas de vivero o arboles del Japón. Ya que estos últimos, tienen de diez a doscientos años, podremos así evitar similar espera para poder disfrutar los placeres que se obtienen mediante la experimentación de técnicas nuevas (¡por la simple razón de que la vida no es muy larga!). A través de nuestro progreso podemos realizar más y más modificaciones detalladas a nuestros árboles para el perfeccionamiento estético. Bonsai es un arte en evolución. Yamadori, la obra de un árbol por medio natural, es un abordamiento al tema, que nos permite trabajar en un árbol que ha sido forjado por la naturaleza.

En conclusión, el simple placer de trabajar con un árbol que me permitirá crecer,es una experiencia de un un valor incalculable.

Este Junípero Chino ya no largo semeja a un Bonsai (fotografia n.1) Despúes de haberme asegurado de su estado óptimo, comencé a restructurarlo completamente, siendo esto el primer paso (fotografia n.2). Una vez reeprendido el crecimiento, fué transplantado y reinstalado (fotografia n.3). El resto fue puesto en manos del tiempo, y seis meses más tarde la metamorfosis continuaba aún.

Este pino pentaphylla (x Kokonge) es un buen ejemplo (fotografia n.4). Si no es podado con cierta regularidad, se transformará en un seto, y perderá su carácter, además de toda su ramificación interior, y al final parecerá más a un cepillo, que a un bonsai. Es el comienzo de Julio, el pino esta en buena forma, y sus raices son vigorosas. La poda para su adelgazamiento es la fase primera en la restructuración del árbol. Ya hemos retirado todos los brotes nuevos dejando los que brotaron dos años más atrás. Durante este verano, la luz del sol penetrará en las ramas internas y con ello reaparecerán capullos nuevos. Esto nos permitirá realizar una segunda selección de ramas antes del alambrado que llevaremos a cabo en Noviembre o Diciembre (fotografia n.5).

Japonaise. Ces derniers ont entre 10 et 200 ans. Cela nous évitera d'attendre aussi longtemps le plaisir d'expérimenter les techniques complémentaires (dans le cas où nous ne vivrons pas aussi longtemps). A travers notre progression nous apporterons à nos bonsaï des modifications de plus en plus pointues pour améliorer leur esthétique. Le bonsaï est un art évolutif. Le Yamadori (prélèvement dans la nature) est une approche qui permet de travailler un arbre de caractère forgé par la nature. En conclusion, seul le plaisir de travailler l'arbre qui me fera grandir vaut d'être vécu.

Le travail effectué pour cet ouvrage montre qu'un arbre même d'origine Japonaise si il n'est pas entretenu ne peut rester une œuvre d'art.

Ce Juniperus chinensis n'a plus rien d'un bonsaï (ph n°1). Après s'être assuré de sa bonne santé, j'ai essayé de le restructurer complètement, ceci a été la première étape (ph n°2). Puis il a été placé au soleil pour faire apparaître les nouvelles pousses sur le vieux bois. Une fois la reprise assurée il est rempoté et repositionné (ph n°3). Il ne reste plus qu'à laisser faire le temps, et dans six mois environ continuer sa métamorphose.

Ce pinus pentaphylla var Kokonoe (ph n°4) en est un bel exemple, si il n'est pas taillé régulièrement il devient trop touffu, perd son caractère et ressemble plus à un buisson qu'un bonsaï et la ramification interne meurt. Le pin est en forme, les racines sont vigoureuses; nous sommes début juillet. Cette taille d'éclaircissement est une première phase dans la restructuration de l'arbre, nous avons supprimée les pousses pour revenir aux ramifications vieilles de deux ans, durant l'été le soleil pénétrera dans les branches et fera apparaître de nouveaux bourgeons, cela nous permettra de pouvoir faire une 2eme sélection de branches avant la remise en forme par la ligature en novembre ou décembre (ph n°5).

Bäumen von Japan lernen. Da die letzteren zwischen 10 und 200 Jahren alt sind, können wir vielleicht vermeiden, die gleiche Zeitspanne warten zu müssen, andere Techniken auszuprobieren (für den Fall, daß wir nicht so lange leben!). Durch unseren Fortschritt können wir unsere Bäume mehr und mehr modifizieren und ihre Ästhetik verbessern. Bonsai ist eine sich entfaltende Kunst. Yamadori, das Gestalten von Bäumen aus der Natur, ist eine Annäherung, die uns befähigt mit Bäumen zu arbeiten, die von der Natur gemacht wurden. Die Schlußfolgerung ist - nur die Freude an einem Baum zu arbeiten, der mich selbst wachsen läßt, ist es wert Erfahrungen zu machen.

Dieser chinesische Wacholder (Foto Nr. 1) gleicht nicht mehr einem Bonsai. Nachdem ich mich von seiner Gesundheit überzeugt hatte, versuchte ich ihn vollständig umzugestalten. Dies ist der 1. Schritt (Foto 2). Als das Wachstum wieder einsetzte, wurde er umgetopft und neu positioniert (Foto 3). Das Übrige wird die Zeit tun, in sechs Monaten wird die Umgestaltung weitergehen.

Diese fünfnadlige Kiefer (x Kokonge) ist ein gutes Beispiel (Foto 4) dafür, daß sie zu buschig wird, wenn sie nicht regelmäßig ausgeputzt wird. Sie verliert ihren Charakter, die innere Verästelung und sieht zum Schluß mehr wie Busch als ein Bonsai aus. Es ist Anfang Juli, die Kiefer ist in guter Form und hat kfäfitge Wurzeln. Dieses Ausdünnen ist die erste phase, den Baum neu zu struktuieren. Wir haben alle jungen Triebe bis auf sas zweijährige (zurückliegende) Wachstum entfernt. Wahrend des Sommers kann das Sonnenlicht in das Innere des Baumes eindringen und neue Knospen werden erscheinen. Dadurch können wir noch ein Zweites Mal die Äste auswählen, bevor wir im November oder Dezember drahten (Foto 5).

◀ **Prunus mume**
⇕ 45cm
Japan 1993
▭ Japan

▶ **Acer buergerianum**
⇕ 95cm
Japan 1993
▭ Korea

DENMARK

Jørgen Skammeritz

Jørgen Skammeritz is a 43-year old from Denmark who bonsai people have already nicknamed "The Viking". He has been engaged in bonsai, his big hobby, for the past 10 years and five years ago he opened a shop called "Bonsai Galleriet". For the past 4 years he has studied regularly with Dan Barton, who is his main inspiration, mainly because of Dan's great sense of aesthetics.

The material Jørgen works on is mainly European yamadori including, among other species, beautiful pines from Norway. He is very concerned with wiring all his trees, and many outstanding bonsai people complement him highly on this. He is also great advocate of education. To use his own words: "We have to teach the members of our bonsai societies to create nice trees, so that they get the same pleasure from this wonderful hobby as the fanatic wirers".

Jørgen Skammeritz holds lectures and workshops at his shop. The lectures are attended by Danish enthusiasts as well as many from the rest of Scandinavia.

For the past few years he has been travelling a lot in Denmark and Norway conducting demonstrations and workshops, and he will be attending "The Joy of Bonsai '98" arranged by Dan Barton in the UK. His bonsai friends consider him a very good teacher with a great sense of humour. On the educational side he has written two best selling books in Danish; My Japanese Garden and Bonsai – 500 Good Tips and Advice.

Jørgen Skammeritz is a member of the board of both EBA and The Danish Bonsai Society. When you visit Bonsai Galleriet in Denmark, you will realise that there are always a lot of enthusiasts around who want help and inspire.

Jørgen Skammeritz, danese di quarantatreanni, è stato soprannominato da altri appassionati di bonsai "Il vichingo", è membro del consiglio dell'EBA e del Dansk Bonsai Selskapet. Da oltre dieci anni coltiva bonsai e da cinque ha aperto un negozio chiamato 'Bonsai Galleriet'. Negli ultimi quattro anni ha studiato regolarmente con Dan Barton, il cui senso estetico è per lui fonte di continua ispirazione.

I materiali sui quali Jørgen lavora sono soprattutto yamadori europei, in particolar modo alcuni bellissimi pini Norvegesi. E' famoso per essere molto attento e scrupoloso nell'applicazione del filo, e questo gli viene riconosciuto da famosi esperti di bonsai. Grande sostenitore della didattica, dice "dobbiamo insegnare ai soci dei nostri Club a creare belle piante in modo che li soddisfino"

Presso il suo negozio e in tutta la Danimarca Jørgen Skammeritz tiene conferenze e dimostrazioni seguite da molti danesi e da persone provenienti da tutta la Scandinavia e sarà presente alla manifestazione 'The Joy of Bonsai '98' organizzato da Dan Barton in Inghilterra. Quando visiterete il Bonsai Galleriet in Danimarca, vi accorgerete che sono veramente tanti gli appassionati desiderosi di imparare. I suoi amici bonsaisti lo considerano un'ottimo insegnate con un grande senso dell'umorismo. Ha scritto inoltre due libri best-seller in Danese; My Japanese Garden e Bonsai - 500 buoni consigli e trucchi.

▲ **Pinus parviflora**

⇕ 40cm ◁▷ 50cm

± 56 years / jahre / anni / ans / años

Dan Barton

Jørgen Skammeritz es un Danés de 43 años al que los aficionados de bonsai le han apodado como "El Vikingo". Ha estado trabajando con los bonsais, su gran pasatiempo desde hace 10 años y hace cinco años inaguró una tienda: "Bonsai Galleriet". En los últimos 4 años ha estudiado con regularidad con Dan Barton, el cual es su mayor inspirador, debido a su gran sentido de la estética.

El material con que Jørgen trabaja es en su mayor parte yamadori europeo incluyendo, entre otras especies, bellos pinos de Noruega. El alambra todos sus árboles concienzudamente, y varias personas importantes del bonsai, le alaban en este aspecto. El es además un gran partidiario de la educación. Tal como él dijo: "Debemos enseñar a los miembros de nuestras sociedades de bonsai como crear arboles bellos, de este modo obtendrán el mismo placer de este pasatiempo tan maravilloso, como los alambristas fanáticos".

Jørgen Skammeritz da conferencias y talleres en su establecimiento. Sus conferencias son atendidas por entusiastas daneses además de un gran número procedentes del resto de Escandinavia.

En los últimos años, él ha estado viajando por Dinamarca y Noruega, acudirá a "The Joy of Bonsai '98" organizado por Dan Barton en el Reino Unido. Sus amigos afiliados a bonsai le consideran un buen profesor con un gran sentido del humor. En la parte educativa , Jørgen, ha escrito dos libros con mucha popularidad en danés; Mi jardín japonés y Bonsai - 500 Buenas ideas y Consej os.

Jørgen Skammeritz es miembro de las j untas de ambas, EBA y La Sociedad Danesa de Bonsai. Cuando uno visita Galerías de Bonsai en Dinamarca, siempre se puede apreciar alrededor un gran número de entusiastas en busca de ayuda e inspiración.

Jørgen Skammeritz est un Danois de 43 ans. Les amateurs de bonsaï le surnomment 'le Viking». Il s'occupe de bonsaï, son passe temps favori, depuis 10 ans. Il y a 5 ans, il a ouvert sa boutique, la «Bonsaï Galleriet». Depuis 4 ans, il étudie avec Dan Barton. Dan est sa source d' inspiration principale, parcequ'il possède un grand sens de l'esthétique.

La matière brute sur laquelle Jørgen travaille consiste principalement en bonsaïs européens recueillis dans la nature, et parmi d'autres espèces, des pins de Norvège magnifiques. Il ligature tous ses arbres et les professionnels du bonsaï le complimentent souvent sur sa technique. Il est partisan de l'education. «Nous devons enseigner aux membres de nos clubs de bonsaï comment créer de beaux arbres pour qu'ils prennent autant de plaisir à ce passe temps merveilleux que les fanatiques du ligaturage».

Jørgen Skammeritz donne des cours et mène des ateliers dans sa boutique. Ses cours sont suivis par d'enthousiastes Danois et aussi des gens venus de toute la Scandinavie. Ces dernières années, il a voyagé à travers tout le Danemark et la Norvège pour organiser des démonstrations et des ateliers. Il assistera aussi à l'évènement «The Joy of Bonsai» organisé par Dan Barton au Royaume Uni. Ses amis amateurs de bonsaï le disent être un bon professeur avec un sens de l'humour. Il a écrit deux livres très populaires en Danois: «Mon jardin Japonais» et «Les Bonsais – 500 trucs et conseils».

Jørgen Skammeritz est membre du comité d'administration de EBA et de la Société Danoise de Bonsai. Quand vous irez à la «Bonsaï Galleriet», vous verrez qu'il y a là-bas toujours un grand nombre d'amateurs de bonsaï prêts à vous aider et qui seront une source d'inspiration.

Jorgen Skammeritz ist ein 43-jähriger Däne, den die Bonsaileute den Spitznamen 'Der Wikinger' gegeben haben. Er beschäftigt sich mit seinem großen Hobby Bonsai seit zehn Jahren und hat vor fünf Jahren ein Geschäft namens 'Bonsai Galleriet' eröffnet. Die letzten vier Jahre hat er regelmäßig bei Dan Barton, seinem Hauptinspirator, studiert und zwar hauptsächlich wegen Dans großem Gefühl für Ästhetik.

Das Material mit dem Jorgen arbeitet, sind meistens europäische Yamadori, darunter, neben anderen Arten, wunderschöne Kiefern aus Norwegen. Er ist sehr darum bemüht, alle seine Bäume zu drahten, was ihm hohes Lob von anderen Bonsaifachleuten einbringt. Außerdem ist er ein großer Fürsprecher für das Unterrichten. Hier seine eigenen Worte: Wir müssen die Mitglieder unserer Bonsaiorganisationen lehren, wie man schöne Bäume gestaltet, damit sie die gleiche Freeude an ihrem Hobby haven wie die fanatischen Drahter.

In seinem Geschäft hält Jorgen Skammeritz Vorträge und Workshops. Seine Vorträge werden sowohl von dänischen Bonsailiebhabern als auch von anderen Skandinaviern besucht. In den letzten Jahren ist er viel in Dänemark und Norwegen herumgereist, um Demonstrationen und Workshops zu geben. Nächstes Jahr wird er bei dem von Dan Barton arrangierten 'The Joy of Bonsai 1998', in Großbritannien dabei sein. Seine Bonsaifreunde halten ihm für einen sehr guten Lehrer mit großem Sinn für Humor. Er hat zwei Bestseller in Dänisch geschrieben: 'Mein japanischer Garten'. Wenn Sie die Bonsai Galleriet in Dänemark besuchen, werden Sie feststellen, daß dort immer eine große Anzahl von Bonsailiebhavern anwesend ist, die Hilfe und Inspiration suchen.

Bonsai Galleriet

Jørgen Skammeritz
Bonsai Galleriet, Skovdalsvej 6,
8260 Viby J., Denmark
Tel: 0045 86 11 80 99
Fax: 0045 86 11 80 99

Jørgen Skammeritz

THE IMPORTANCE OF WIRING

I think that wiring is essential when you want to create a certain image to your trees. In Denmark and in many other countries I have noticed that not many enthusiasts wire their trees. My mentor and good friend, Dan Barton, to whom I am deeply indebted for the way he has opened my mind to bonsai, says: "Wire all branches to the smallest tips even if you have to cut off the branches afterwards!" When you start with your material, whether it comes from a nursery or nature, you have an idea about the structure you want to impose on it. You should always build up the image following the lines of the trunk. With this in mind you should avoid wiring the trunk from the ground to the lowest branch. The crown of the tree should be the part you work on.

To illustrate this principle I have chosen before and after pictures of two Juniperus squamata "Blue Star", a type of material that anybody can get hold of. They come from the same nursery and are both 25 years old. The trunk is 4-5 cm in diameter and the height is 50-60 cm.

I always clean small dead shoots, flakes of loose bark etc. from the branches. You have to take your time to do this job well before you start wiring. I mainly work with aluminium wire, but copper wire tends to hold the branches of conifers in position better. But when you start to practise wiring, choose aluminium as it is the easiest material to work with. When wiring the crown of the tree you can choose different angles of approach. But bear in mind that you do not want to create an aluminium tree but a tree well-wired with aluminium. When wiring the primary branches I often work from one side of the tree to the other in order to create a more natural flow of the thickest wire. Like this I work my way to the top. When wiring the secondary branches I work within a certain foliage pad.

Some of my friends sometimes just wire the trunk and some of the main

L'IMPORTANZA DELLA FILO

Credo che l'applicazione del filo sia essenziale quando si vuole creare un certa immagine nei vostri alberi. In Danimarca ed in altri paesi ho notato che non molti appassionati applicano il filo ai loro alberi. Il mio maestro e buon amico Dan Barton, al quale sarò eternamente grato per avermi aperto la mente al bonsai, dice: "Metti il filo su tutti i rami fino a raggiungere quelli più sottili e non ti preoccupare se dopo ne dovrai tagliare qualcuno!". Quando lavorate un materiale per la prima volta, ovunque sia la sua provenienza, da vivaio o natura che sia, cercate di avere un'idea circa la struttura con la quale la volete impostare, cercando sempre di costruire l'immagine seguendo le linee del tronco. Con questa idea in mente dovreste evitare di applicare il filo sul tronco e quindi lavorare soltanto sulla chioma.

Per illustrare questo principio ho scelto due sequenze di foto di alcuni Juniperus squamate 'Blue Star', una specie reperibile ovunque. Queste due piante provengono dallo stesso vivaio e hanno entrambe 25 anni. Il tronco ha un diametro di 4-5cm ed un'altezza di 50-60cm.

Pulisco sempre i rami dai piccoli germogli morti, da squami di corteccia, etc. Ci vuole del tempo per effettuare bene questo lavoro prima di iniziare l'applicazione del filo. Lavoro principalmente con del filo di alluminio, ma il filo di rame riesce a tenere meglio in posizione i rami del conifera. Quando cominciate ad esercitarvi è meglio scegliere quello di alluminio in quanto è molto più facile da usare. Quando si mette il filo si può partire da vari punti senza mai scordare però che quello che vogliamo ottenere non è un albero d'alluminio ma un albero in cui il filo è stato applicato correttamente. Quando applico il filo ai primi rami lavoro partendo da un lato dell'albero all'altro per creare un flusso naturale del filo più spesso. Lavoro così fino in cima. Quando applico il filo ai rami secondari lavoro entro una certa zona della chioma.

LA IMPORTANCIA DEL ALAMBRADO

Yo creo que el alambrado, es esencial cuando se quiere crear una cierta imagen para tus árboles. En Dinamarca y en otros diversos paises he podido comprobar que no muchos entusiastas alambran sus arboles. Mi mentor y buen amigo, Dan Barton, a quien estoy profundamente agradecido, por la manera en que ha abierto mi mente con referencia al bonsai, dice: "¡Debemos alambrar todas las ramas hasta las puntas incluso aunque luego se vaya a cortar la rama!" Cuando comenzamos con nuestros materiales, vengan de un vivero o vengan de la foresta, se tiene una idea previa sobre la estructura que queremos imponer sobre él. Debemos pues, siempre construir la imagen siguiendo las lineas del tronco. Con esto presente, deberemos evitar el alambrado del tronco desde el suelo hasta la rama más baja. La copa del árbol es la parte que debe trabajarse.

Para ilustrar este principio, he elegido fotografías anteriores y posteriores de dos Juniperus squamata "Blue star", los cuales son el tipo de material de fácil obtención. Proceden ambos del mismo vivero y tienen 25 años. El tronco es 4-5cm de diámetro y su altura es de unos 50-60cm.

Yo siempre limpio los brotes muertos, las escamas de corteza sueltas, etc, de las ramas. Se debe siempre prestar tiempo para hacer este trabajo bien hecho antes de comenzar con el alambrado. Yo trabajo principalmente con alambre de aluminio, pero el alambre de cobre tiende a sujetar las ramas de las coníferas en su debida posición, mejor. Pero cuando se empieza a practicar el alambrado, es mejor elegir aluminio por su fácil manejabilidad. Cuando se alambra la copa del árbol uno debe de escojer diferentes ángulos de enfoque pero es importante recordar que no queremos crear un árbol de aluminio, pero sí un árbol bién alambrado con aluminio. Cuando se comienza el alambrado de las ramas primarias, yo muy amenudo trabajo desde un extremo del árbol hasta otro, para de esta manera crear un movimiento más natural de el alambre más grueso. De este modo busco mi camino hasta el ápice. Cuando se alambran las ramas secundarias hay que trabajar

L'IMPORTANCE DU LIGATURAGE

Je crois que le ligaturage est essentiel lorsqu'on veut créer une certaine image de nos arbres. Au Danemark, et dans beaucoup d'autres pays, j'ai remarqué que peu d'amateurs ligaturent leurs arbres. Mon mentor et ami Dan Barton, à qui je dois beaucoup pour la façon dont il m'a initié à l'art du bonsaï, dit: «Ligaturez toutes les branches jusqu' aux plus petites ramifications, même si vous devez couper ces mêmes branches après!» Quand on commence à travailler sur la matière première choisie, qu' elle vienne de la nature ou d'une pépinière, on a une idée de la forme qu'on veut lui donner. Il faut toujour choisir l'image principale en suivant les lignes du tronc. Ceci dit, on évite de ligaturer le tronc du sol à la branche la plus basse. Par contre, on doit ligaturer la couronne de l'arbre.

Pour illustrer ce principe, j'ai choisi deux photos, avant et après, représentant deux Juniperus squamata «Etoile bleue», un type d'arbre facile à obtenir. Ils viennent de la même pépinière et ont tous deux vingt cinq ans. Le tronc est de 4 a 5 cm de diamètre et leur taille est de 50 à 60 cm.

Je nettoye bien les branches et j'enlève le bois mort, les morceaux d'écorce décollés etc. Il faut prendre son temps pour préparer l'arbre au ligaturage. Je travaille principalement avec des fils d'aluminium mais les fils de cuivre maintiennent mieux les branches des conifères. Quand on commence à s'entrainer à la technique du ligaturage, l'aluminium est plus facile à manier. Quand on ligature la couronne d'un arbre, on peut choisir plusieurs angles différents. Il ne faut pas oublier qu'on veut créer un arbre ligaturé avec des fils d'aluminium, pas un arbre d'aluminium! Quand je ligature les branches primaires, je travaille d'un côté de l'arbre à l'autre pour obtenir une fluidité plus naturelle des fils les plus epais. De cette facon, je continue jusqu'à la cime. Quand je ligature les branches secondaires, je travaille à l'interieur même des coussinets de feuillage.

DIE WICHTIGKEIT DES DRAHTENS

Ich glaube, daß Drahten dann sehr wichtig ist, wenn Sie ein bestimmtes Bild Ihrer Bäume schaffen wollen. In Dänemark und in vielen anderen Ländern have ich festgestellt, daß nicht viele Bonsailiebhaber ihre Bäume drahten. Mein Mentor und guter Freund Dan Barton, dem ich tief verpflichtet bin für die Art und Weise wie er mire Bonsai nahe gebracht hat, sagt: ' Drahte alle Äste bis in die feinste Verzweigung, selbst wenn Du die Äste später wieder abschneiden mußt'. Wenn Sie mit Ihrem Material anfangen zu arbeiten, egal ob es aus der Bazmschule oder aus der Natur kommt, haben Sie bereits eine Vorstellung welchen Aufbau es haven soll. Sie sollten sich das Bild des Baumes anhand des Stammverlaufes aufbauen. Wenn Sie sich das vergegenwärtigen, sollten Sie vermeiden, den Stamm von der Erdoberfläche bis zum untersten Ast zu drahten. Die krone des Baumes ist der Teil, an dem Sie arbeiten sollten.

Um dieses Prinzip zu erläutern, habe ich von zwei Juniperus squamata 'Blue Star' Bilder von vorher und nachher ausgewählt. Juniperus squamata ist Ausgangsmaterial, das jeder bekommen kann. Beide Bäume kommen aus der selben Baumschule und sind beide 25 jahre alt. Der Stamm misst im Durchmesser 4-5 Zentimeter und die Höhe beträgt 50 - 60 Zentimeter. Ich reinige die Äste immer von kleinen, abgestorbenen Trieben, von losen Rindenteilen, usw. Nehmen Sie sich für diese Arbeit genügend Zeit, bevor Sie mit dem Drahten anfangen.

Hauptsächlich arbeite ich mit Aluminiumdraht, Kupferdraht hält jedoch die Äste von Koniferen besser in der richtigen Position. Wenn Sie jedoch erst anfangen zu drahten, sollten Sie mit Aluminiumdraht arbeiten, er ist leichter zu verarbeiten. Wenn Sie die Krone des Baumes drahten, können Sie zwischen verschiedenen Annäherungswinkeln wählen. Aber denken Sie immer daran, daß Sie keinen Aluminiumbaum erschaffen wollen, sondern einen Baum, der sehr gut gedrahtet ist. Wenn ich die Hauptäste drahte, arbeite ich oft von einer Seite des Baumes zur anderen um einen natürlichen

branches. But consider the fact that it is mainly the silhouette of the tree that you notice then. So in order to see the whole tree and its structure, you need to wire all the branches to put them in their right position. When you look at the two examples, note that it took me a whole day cleaning each tree before wiring it, and then it took me three days to wire each tree.

Good wiring enables you to place all the foliage pads in their exact position – it is the tips of the foliage pads that indicate the flow of the branches. When you decide on the position of the foliage pads make sure they stretch in the same direction throughout the tree.

In my opinion there is nothing worse than a tree which is only half-wired, with some branches in the right position and others completely out of position.

When I apply the wire to the branches, I wire tightly but not too tightly. If there is a lot of air between wire and branch you run the risk of breaking the branch when bending it. When applying two or even three pieces of wire to the same branch, make sure that the wires are close together. If you do not do that, you will get a "spring reaction", and the wire won't do the job.

There are hundreds of good pieces of advice on how to learn to wire. Pick them up and make use of them. Believe me, it takes time. But then again, what is time? The angler will sit in his boat bathing a worm for a whole day without catching anything. But rest assured, he has had a marvellous day anyway. It is the same with the bonsai enthusiast. He will sit for a whole day wiring, but the fulfilment is the moment when he can finally position all the wired branches and twigs. This moment is worth "wiring" for!

Certi miei amici applicano il filo soltanto al tronco ed alcuni rami principali, manon bisogna dimenticare che per far emergere una precisa sihoulette della pianta dobbiamo applicare il filo su tutti i rami , specialmente quelli più sottili. Quando vedrete i due esempi noterete che ho impiegato un giorno intero per pulire ogni albero , successivamente ho impiegato tre giorni per applicare il filo ad ogni albero.

Una correta applicazione del filo ti permette di sistemare tutti le foglie nella loro posizione esatta – è proprio la parte estrema delle foglie che indica la direzione del flusso dei rami. Quando decidi la posizione delle foglie bisogna assicurare che la direzione sia omogenea in ogni parte dell'albero.

Secondo me, non c'è niente di peggio che un'albero cui il filo è stato applicato per metà, con certi rami nella direzione giusta ed altri completamente fuori posto.

Quando applico il filo ai rami, lo fisso stretto ma non troppo stretto. Se viene lasciato troppo spazio tra il filo ed il ramo si rischia di rompere il ramo quando viene piegato. Quando si applica due o tre pezzi di filo allo stesso ramo bisogna assicurare che i fili siano vicini uno all'altro altrimenti avverrà una reazione a 'molla' ed il filo non funzionerà bene.

Ci sono una centinaia di buoni consigli per imparare ad applicare il filo. Ascoltateli e metteteli in pratica. Credetemi, ci vuole del tempo, ma dopo tutto cos'è tempo? Il pescatore rimarrà seduto nella sua barca con l'esca sull'amo per un'intera giornata senza pescare niente. Ma stai tranquillo che lui si è divertito in ogni caso. E' lo stesso concetto per il bonsaista che può stare seduto tutto il giorno ad applicare il filo ma l'appagamento è quando può finalmente posizionare tutti rami e ramoscello. Questo è il momento in cui vale la pena aspettare.

dentro de un grupo de hojas exclusivo.

Algunos de mis compañeros alambran solamente el tronco y algunas de las ramas principales. Pero consideremos el hecho de que será entonces la silueta del árbol lo que veremos. Por lo tanto para poder apreciar el árbol y su estructura completa, se requiere el alambrado de todas las ramas, para de esta manera modelarlas en la posición correcta. Cuando miréis los dos ejemplos, debo de señalar que solamente la limpieza de cada árbol me llevó un dia completo más luego el alambrado que consumió tres dias con cada pieza. El buen alambrado nos permite colocar todos los brotes en su posición exacta – es la punta de los frondes la que indica el movimiento de la rama. Una vez elegida la posición y movimiento de las ramas deberemos de asegurarnos que los demás sigan esta trayectoria.

En mi opinión no hay cosa peor que un árbol medio alambrado, con algunas ramas en la posición correcta y otras sin embargo, completamente desorientadas. Cuando aplico el alambrado a las ramas, las aprieto firmemente pero sin oprimir. Si hay demasiado aire entre el alambre y la rama, esta última corre el peligro de quebrar al ser manipularda. Cuando aplicamos los otros pedazos de alambre en una misma rama, debemos pues de asegurarnos que los alambres esten próximos los unos a los otros. Si fuese asi, el resultado sería una "reacción muelle" y consiguientemente el alambre no cumpliría su labor.

Existen cientos de buenos consejos para el aprendizaje del alambrado. Reunamos todos y usémoslos. Créame, es una labor lenta. Pero por otro lado, ¿Qué es el tiempo? El pescador, se sentará en su barca con el cebo en el agua durante todo un día, para posiblemente no pescar nada. Pero estad seguros que ese ha sido probablemente un día estupendo. Lo mismo ocurre con el estusiasta de bonsai. Permanecerá todo el día sentado alambrando, pero la satisfacción llegará cuando por fín todas las ramas y ramitas estén finalmente situadas en la posición deseada. Por este momento merece la pena todo el alambrado necesario.

Certains de mes amis ligaturent seulement le tronc et les branches principales. Alors, on ne remarque que la silhouette générale de l'arbre. Pour apprécier l'arbre entier et la structure des branches, il faut ligaturer toutes les branches et les mettre dans la bonne position. Regardez ces deux exemples; il a fallu un jour entier pour nettoyer chaque arbre et ensuite trois jours pour ligaturer chacun d'eux.

Une bonne technique de ligaturage permet de placer tous les coussinets de feuillage dans leur position précise. Le bout des rameaux de chaque coussinet donne son mouvement aux branches. Quand on décide de la position de chaque coussinet, il faut s'assurer qu'ils se dirigent tous dans le même sens sur l'ensemble de l'arbre.

Il n'y a rien de pire qu'un arbre ligaturé à moitié, avec certaines branches dans la bonne direction et d'autres non.

Quand je ligature, je ligature serré mais pas trop. S'il y a trop d'espace entre les fils et la branche, on risque de la casser en la pliant. Si on utilise deux ou trois fils sur la même branche, il faut s'assurer qu'ils sont proches les uns des autres. Sinon, on a un «effet ressort», et les fils n'auront pas l'effet voulu.

On pourrait donner des centaines de bons conseils sur le ligaturage. Il faut apprendre les techniques et ensuite les utiliser régulièrement. Croyez-moi, ça prend du temps! Mais après tout, qu'est ce que le temps? Un pêcheur peut rester assis dans sa barque une journée entière à faire flotter un ver dans l'eau, et ne rien attraper. Mais, soyez sans inquiétude, il aura passé une excellente journée. C' est pareil pour l'amateur de bonsaï. Il peut passer une journée entière à ligaturer son arbre, et le meilleur moment pour lui arrive quand il peut enfin mettre toutes les branches en place. Un tel moment vaut la peine d'avoir ligaturé toute une journée!

verlauf des dicksten Drahtes zu schaffen. So arbeite ich mich bis zur Spitze hoch. Beim Drahtender untergeordneten Äste arbeite ich an einem bestimmten Nadelposlter.

Einige meiner Freunde drahten machmal nur den Stamm und einige der Hauptäste. Sie sollten aber bedenken, daß Sie später nur die Silhouette des Baumes sehen. Wenn Sie aber den ganzen Baum in seinem Aufbau sehen möchten, müssen Sie alle Äste drahten, um sie in die richtige Position zu bringen. Wenn Sie sich die beiden Beispiele ansehen, sollten Sie wissen, daß ich jeden Baum einen ganzen Tag lang säuberte , für jeden Baum brachte ich dann drei Tage zum Drahten.

Gutes Drahten befähigt Sie, die Laub- oder Nadelpolster in ihre exakte Position zu bringen an den Spitzen der Polster zeigt sich der Verlauf der Äste. Wenn Sie die Polster positionieren, sollten Siedarauf achten, daß sie sich am ganzen Baum immer in die gleiche Richtung strecken. Meiner Ansicht nach gibt es nichts Schlimmeres als ein halbgedrahteter Baum, an dem einige Äste in der richtigen Position sind, die anderen dagegen total unpositioniert.

Wenn ich den Draht an den Ästen anlege, drahte ich eng, jedoch nicht zu eng. Wenn zwischen dem Ast und dem Draht zuviel Hohlraum ist, kann man ihm beim Biegen brechen. Wenn ein Ast zwei-oder gar dreimal gedrahtet werden muß, sollten die Drähte dicht beieinander liegen. Wenn Sich nicht darauf achten, entsteht eine 'Federungseffekt' und die Drähte nützen nichts. Es gibt hunderte von guten Ratschlägen, wie man das Drahten erlernt. Lernen sie die Ratschläge und wenden Sie sie an. Glauben Sie mir, es braucht Zeit. Andererseits, was ist Zeit?

Der Angler sitzt in seinem Boot und badet den ganzen Tag einen Wurm, ohne etwas zu fangen. Aber Sie können sicher sein, daß er trotzdem einen wunderbaren Tag hatte. So ist es auch mit Bonsailiebhabern. Er sitzt einen ganzen Tag da und drahtet, die Erfüllung ist der Moment, wenn er alle gedrahteten Äste und Zweige positionieren kann. Dieser Augenblick ist das Drahten wert!

◄ **Taxus baccata**
⇕ 65cm ◄▷ 40cm
± 37 years / jahre / anni / ans / años
Yamadori 1993
⌐⊐ Jørgen Skammeritz

▲ **Pyracantha augustifolia**

⇕ 23cm   ◁▷ 24cm

± 25 years / jahre / anni / ans / años

⬭ Tokoname

▲ **Prunus spinosa**

⇕ 23cm ◁▷ 35cm

± 68 years / jahre / anni / ans / año

Yamadori 1994

▭ Dan Barton

▲ **Ilex crenata**

⬍ 60cm   ◁▷ 50cm

± 52 years / jahre / anni / ans / años

Nursery / baumschule / vivaio /

Luis Vallejo

GB

Luis Vallejo García Mauriño was born in Madrid in 1957, the son of a forester, in whose nursery he played as a child. He studied horticulture at the Escuela Técnica Superior de Ingenieros Agrónomos in Madrid, and now works as a landscape architect. He has been growing bonsai now for over twenty years – his first masters being the books he found in the family library: The Masters Book of Bonsai and Saikei: Living Landscapes in Miniature. Being self-taught, his progress was slow until he attended courses John Naka, Saburo Kato and Masahiko Kimura.

Since 1985 Luis has been giving lectures, demonstrations and workshops at home and abroad. His articles have appeared in magazines in several countries and he has also published a monograph on Fagus sylvatica.

In his professional capacity, as well as planning parks and gardens, he has also designed and constructed dedicated bonsai display areas at the Moncloa Palace, Madrid; the Royal Botanic Gardens, Madrid; the Municipal Bonsai Museum, Alcobendas, Madrid; Display of suiseki at the bonsai arboretum, Boswil, Switzerland. He is now working on the display facility at the Royal Botanic Gardens, Madrid.

Other activities have included:
• Curator of the collection of ex-Prime Minister Felipe González (1987 - 1996), currently in its new home at the Centre of Advanced Scientific Studies of the Ministry of Education and Science.
• Consultant to the collection of the Palace of Zarzuela
• Collecting from the Atlas Mountains for King Hassan of Morocco.

His personal collection consists mainly of native species (Pinus sylvestris, Pinus uncinata, Juniperus sabina, Acer campestre, Taxus baccata) as well as Japanese maples by artists such as Kato, Kaneko, Takeyama, Nakajima, Hamano.

Luis Vellejo Garcia Mauriño è nato a Madrid nel 1957, figlio di un forestale. Fin da piccolo giocava nel vivaio nel quale lavorava il padre. Ha studiato orticultura alla Scuola Tecnica Superiore di Ingeneria Agronoma a Madrid e ora lavora come architetto paesaggista. Ha coltivato bonsai per più di vent'anni ed i suoi maestri iniziali furono i libri trovati nella biblioteca di famiglia. Essendo un autodidatta la sua abilità tecnina progredi molto lentamente finchè non frequentò corsi con John Naka, Saburo Kato e Masahiko Kimura.

Dal 1985 Luis tiene lezioni, dimostrazioni e seminari a casa sua ed all'estero. I suoi articoli sono apparsi su riviste in molti paesi e ha pubblicato una monografia sul Fagus sylvatica. Oltre a pianificare parchi e giardini, la sua capacità professionale lo ha portato a disegnare e costruire zone di esposizione dedicate al bonsai nel palazzo Moncloa a Madrid; il Real Jardín Botánico a Madrid; il Museo Municipal de Bonsai ad Alcobendas, Madrid; mostra di suiseki all'arboretum di bonsai a Boswil, Svizzera. Ora sta lavorando all'allestimento di una mostre al Real Jardín Botánico, Madrid.

Altra su attività includono:
• curatore della collezione dell'ex Primo Ministro Felipe Gonzalez (1987-1996) che si trova attualmente nel Centro di Studi Scientifici Avanzati del Ministero di Educazione e Scienza
• Consulente della collezione presso il palazzo di Zarzuela.
• Ha raccolto piante, dalla montagne Atlas, per conto del Re Hassan di Marocco.

La sua collezione personale consiste principalmente in specie spagnole (Pinus sylvestris, Pinus uncinata, Juniperus sabina, Acer campestre, Taxus baccata) oltre ad aceri giapponesi di artisti quali Kato, Kaneko, Takeyama, Nakajima, Hamano.

Fagus sylvatica
⇕ 50cm
Yamadori 1988
Tokoname Hirano

Nace en Madrid en febrero de 1957, de padre arboricultor. Sus juegos infantiles se desarrollan en el vivero familiar. Finaliza sus estudios primarios e ingresa en la Escuela Técnica Superior de Ingenieros Agrónomos de Madrid. Su profesión es Paisajista. Cultiva Bonsai desde hace más de veinte años; sus primeros maestros son unos libros que encuentra en la biblioteca familiar: 'The masters book of Bonsai', y 'Saikei: Living Landscapes in Miniature'. Sus lentos comienzos como autodidacta acaban cuando asiste a cursos, demostraciones y exposiciones con J Naka, S Kato, M Kimura. Da conferencias, demostraciones y talleres desde 1985 en toda españa y en otros paises. Ha publicado o aparecido en revistas especializadas.

Ha publicado una monografía sobre las hayas. Dentro de su actividad profesional de proyectos de parques, jardines públicos y privados, proyecta distintos espacios para exponer bonsai:

• Pabellón para Exposición de Bonsai en el Palacio de la Moncloa, Madrid; Exposición Real Jardín Botánico Madrid.

• 1994/1995: Museo Municipal de Bonsai en Alcobendas, Madrid.

• 1995 Expositores de piedra para el Miniarboretum de Boswil (Suiza). Actualmente desarrolla el anteproyecto para la Colección Permanente de Bonsai en el Real Jardín Botánico de Madrid.

• Conservador 1987-1996 de la Colección de Felipe González en el Palacio de la Moncloa.

• Conservador de ésta misma colección, donada al Centro Superior de Investigaciones Científicas, del Ministerio de Educación y Ciencia, hasta la actualidad.

• Asesor de la Colección del Palacio de la Zarzuela.

• Recuperación de arboles en la Cordillera del Atlas para S M Hassan II de Marruecos.

Su colección está compuesta principalmente por arboles autóctonos españoles (Pinus sylvestris, Pinus uncinata, Juniperus sabina, Acer campestre, Taxus baccata) y arces japoneses de los artistas S Kato, N Kaneko, Takeyama, Nakajima, Hamano).

Luis Vallejo Garcia Mauriño est né à Madrid en 1957. C'est le fils d'un forestier. Il joua dans la pépinière de son père pendant son enfance. Il étudia l'horticulture à l'Escuela Tecnica Superior de Ingenieros Agronomos à Madrid et travaille à present comme architecte paysagiste. Il fait pousser des bonsaïs depuis plus de vingt ans - ses premiers maîtres furent les livres trouvés dans la bibliothèque familiale: le Livre des Maîtres de Bonsaï et de Saikei: Paysage Miniatures Vivants. Etant autodidacte, son progrès fut lent jusqu'au moment où il commença à suivre les cours de John Naka, Saburo Kato et Masahiko Kimura.

Depuis 1985, Luis donne des cours, organise des démonstrations, des ateliers en Espagne et à l'etranger. Ses articles sont publiés dans plusieurs pays, il a aussi publié une monographie sur les Fagus sylvatica.

Sur le plan professionnel, il planifie des parcs, des jardins, mais a aussi dessiné et construit des stands d'exhibition consacrés aux bonsaïs au Palais Moncloa à Madrid; aux Jardins Botaniques Royaux à Madrid; au Musée Municipal de Bonsaïs à Alcobendas, à Madrid; à l'Exhibition de Suiseki à l'arboretum de bonsaï de Boswil en Suisse. Il travaille en ce moment sur l'exhibition des Jardins Botaniques Royaux à Madrid.

Il est aussi:

• Conservateur de la collection de l'ex-Premier Ministre Felipe Gonzales (1987-1996), à present au Centre d'Etudes Scientifiques Avancées du Ministère de l'Education et de la Science.

• Conseillé à la Collection du Palais de Zarzuela.

• Collecteur d'arbres dans les montagnes de l'Atlas pour le roi Hassan du Maroc.

Sa collection personnelle est composée principalement d'arbres de son pays (Pinus sylvestris, Pinus uncinata, Juniperus sabina, Acer campestre, Taxus baccata) ainsi que des érables du Japon crées par des artistes tels que Kato, Kaneko, Takeyama, Nakajima, Hamano.

Luis Vallejo Garcia Mauriño, Sohn eines Försters wurde 1957 in Madrid geboren. Als Kind spielte er in der Baumschule seines Vaters. Er studierte Gartenbau an der Escuela Tecnica Superior de Ingenieros Agronomos in Madrid und arbeitet jetzt als Landschaftsarchitekt. Seit über 20 Jahren zieht er jetzt Bonsai - seine ersten Lehrmeister waren die Bücher, die er in der Familienbibliothek fand, so z-B. 'The Masters Book of Bonsai' und 'Saikei, Living Landscapes in Miniature'. Als Autodidakt war sein Fortschritt langsam, bis er an Kursen von John Naka, Saburo Kato und Mashiko Kimura teilnahm. Seit 1985 gibt Luis Vorträge, Demanstrationen und Workshops daheim und im Ausland. Seine Artikel sind in verschiedenen Ländern in Magazinen erschienen und er hat auch über die Fagus sylvatica eine Monographie veröffentlicht.

In seiner professionellen Fähigkeit, wie auch bei der Planung von Parks und Gärten, hat er auch Bonsai-Ausstellungsgelände im 'Moncloa Palast in Madrid', den 'Königlichen Botanischen Gärten' in Madrid und im 'Municipal Bonsai Museum, Alcobendas' ebenfalls in Madrid, geplant und erbaut. Auch für die Ausstellung von Suiseki im Arboretum in Boswil ist er verantwortlich. Zur Zeit arbeitet er an den Ausstellungsanlagen des 'Königlichen Botanischen Gartens' in Madrid.

Andere Aktivitäten beinhalten folgendes:

• Kurator der Sammlung des Expremierministers Felipe Gonzalez (1987-1996) die gegenwärtig in ihrer neuen Heimat, dem 'Zentrum für fortschrittliche, wissenschaftliche Studien' auch 'Ministerium für Erziehung und Wissenschaft' genannt.

• Beratender Spezialist der Sammlung des Zarzuela-Palastes.

• Yamadori-Sammler im Atlasgebirge für König Hassan von Marokko.

Seine persönliche Sammlung besteht hauptsächlich aus heimischen Arten (Pinus sylvestris, Pinus uncinata, Juniperus sabina, Acer campestre, Taxus baccata). Außerdem sammelt er japanische Ahorne von Künstlern vie Kato, kaneko, Takayama, Nakajima und Hamano.

Luis Vallejo
Loira 4, 28707 S.S. de los Reyes, Madrid, Spain
Tel: 0034 1 657 0954
Fax: 0034 1 657 0954

Luis Vallejo

BONSAI – TOTAL ART

It is easy to forget that the art of bonsai is not limited to the principal object – the tree – but includes all the associated objects. When we grow and display a bonsai, we must consider its height, size, colour, texture, movement, as well as accent plants. We must consider the background against which the trees are displayed, the area in which they are exhibited and the spaces between them. Combining all these elements well creates a harmonic entity. One cannot establish rules to achieve this. We must consider the following basic, interdependent principles.

1 **Hierarchy** One must be aware of the order of the various elements, avoiding competition between them: tree - table - accent plants - suiseki - other trees

The tree, first in the hierarchy, governs the other elements which are subordinated by its volume, colour, movement. Also, different parts of the tree (trunk, branches, leaves, flowers) are subject to this hierarchical relationship according to quantitative factors such as thickness and length but, above all, are determined by qualitative factors: proportion, colour, texture, form.

A hierarchy does not mean some elements are less important. Any element could have a decisive role in the composition: balance, counterpoise or to set the scene. Even a minor disruption to the hierarchical order affects the entire composition. An extreme example would be choosing a visually heavy pot for a slender tree. The pot would not complement the tree because hierarchically it is out of place.

2 **Scale** The art of bonsai is not only a scaled reproduction of nature. It is a symbolic representation or abstraction of nature in miniature. All elements must function together in the same scale. Choosing accent plants with leaves larger than those of the tree they are supposed to complement would destroy the sensation of scale of the whole. This proportion-

BONSAI – ARTE TOTALE

E'semplice dimenticare che l'arte bonsai non è limitata all'oggetto principale. cioè l'albero, ma comprende anche tutti gli oggetti associati. Quando coltiviamo e mostriamo un bonsai dobbiamo considerare la sua altezza, dimensioni, colore, consistenza, movimento nonchè le piante di compagnia. Dobbiamo considerare lo sfondo contro il quale viene esposto l'albero, l'area nella quale viene mostrato e gli spazi fra di loro.

Unendo bene tutti questi elementi si crea un'entità armoniosa. Non si possono stabilire delle regole per ottenere ciò ma dobbiamo considerare i seguenti principi basilari ed interdipendenti.

1 **Gerarchia** Bisogna essere consapevoli dell'ordine dei vari elementi, evitando la concorrenza tra di loro: albero - tavolo - piante di compagnia - suiseki - altri alberi.

L'albero, primo nella gerarchia, controlla gli altri elementi che subiscono il suo volume, colore, movimento. Inoltre, diverse parti dell'albero (tronco, rami, foglie, fiori) sono soggetti a questo rapporto gerarchico a seconda dei fattori qualitativi quali proporzione, colore, consistenza, forma.

Questa gerarchia non intende dire che alcuni elementi sono meno importanti di altri. Qualsiasi elemento potrebbe avere un ruolo decisivo nella composizione, in equilibrio, o contrapposto o per completare la scena. Anche un'interruzione minore nell'ordine di gerarchia potrebbe influire sull'intera composizione. Un esempio estremo sarebbe di scegliere un vaso pesante per un albero snello. Il vaso non completerebbe l'albero perchè è in modo gerarchico fuori posto.

2 **Scala** L'arte del bonsai non è soltanto una riproduzione della natura in scala ma è una rappresentazione ad astrazione di natura in miniatura. Scegliendo le piante di compagnia con foglie più grandi di quelle dell'albero, che dovrebbero andarlo a completare, si rovinerebbe la sensazione

BONSAI - ARTE INTEGRAL

Muchas veces se olvida que el bonsai es un arte, que no sólo se limita al árbol, objeto principal pero no único del bonsai, sino además a todo lo que le rodea complementándolo.

Cuando cultivamos y/o exponemos un bonsai, se debe tener en cuenta desde el expositor donde lo colocamos; su altura, dimensión, textura, color, movimiento, etc hasta las plantas de acento, los fondos expositivos, los arboles que son expuestos, el vacío entre ellos y el espacio que los contienen. El relacionar bien todos los elementos hace que la escala funcione consiguiendo una impresión o sensación armónica en el conjunto. Para conseguir esto, no se pueden establecer unas reglas fijas, habrá que tener en cuenta los siguientes principios básicos (principios que son interdependientes).

1 **Jerarquía** Debe estar muy claro el orden de importancia entre los distintos elementos evitando la competencia entre ellos: árbol - mesa expositiva - plantas de acento - suiseki - otros arboles.

El árbol, primero en esta jerarquía condiciona a los demás elementos estando estos supeditados a las características de volúmen, color, movimiento. Incluso las distintas partes del árbol: tronco, ramas, hojas, flores, frutos, están sujetos a esta relación jerárquica por factores cuantitativos como por ejemplo grosores, longitudes, y sobre todo, viene determinado por los factores cualitativos:proporción, textura, color, forma.

Este orden jerárquico no significa que haya elementos de menor importancia, ya que cualquiera puede tener una importancia decisiva en la composición: equilibrio, complementariedad o aportación de matiz. Una pequeña alteración en este orden jerárquico afecta a la totalidad de la composición. Un ejemplo exagerado sería una elección de maceta con relieve para un árbol ligero. La maceta no complementaría al árbol, puesto que se ha situado en un lugar que no corresponde.

2 **Escala** El arte del bonsai no es sólo

BONSAI – UN ART TOTAL

Il est facile d'oublier que l'art du bonsaï n'est pas limité à l'objet principal – l'arbre – mais inclus aussi tous les autres objets qui lui sont associés. Quand on fait pousser un arbre et qu'on l'exhibe, il faut prendre en compte sa hauteur, sa taille, sa couleur, sa texture, son mouvement, mais aussi les plantes «accent». Il faut prendre en compte le fond sur lequel les arbres sont exhibés, l'endroit, et les espaces entre les arbres. Lorsque ces éléments sont bien associés, une entité harmonieuse se crée. On ne peut pas imposer de règles pour y arriver. On doit tenir compte des principes interdépendants suivants:

1 La hiérarchie On doit connaitre la place des éléments dans la hiérarchie et éviter la competition entre eux: l'arbre – la table – les plantes «accent» – les suiseki - les autres arbres.

L'arbre, premier dans la hiérarchie, gouverne tous les autres éléments qui lui sont subordonnés, à cause de son volume, sa couleur, son mouvement. Aussi, certaines parties de l'arbre (le tronc, les branches, les feuilles, les fleurs) sont aussi sujettes à cette relation hiérarchique d'après des facteurs de proportions comme l'épaisseur et la longueur mais, par dessus tout, sont determinées par des facteurs de quantité: la proportion, la couleur, la texture, la forme.

Une hiérarchie ne veut pas dire que certains éléments soient moins importants que d'autres. Tout élément peut avoir un rôle décisif dans la composition: l'équilibre, le contre-poids, la mise en scène. Même un petit changement de l'ordre hiérarchique affecte toute la composition. Un exemple extrême consisterait à choisir un pot lourd visuellement pour un arbre fin. Le pot ne complète pas l'arbre car il n'est pas à sa place dans la hiérarchie.

2 L'échelle L'art bonsaï est non seulement une reproduction à l'échelle de la nature. C'est une représentation symbolique, une abstraction de la nature en miniature. Tous les éléments doivent fonc-

BONSAI – TOTALE KUNST

Man vergizt leicht, daß die Bonsaikunst nicht auf das hauptsächliche Objekt - dem Baum - begrenzt ist, sondern auch die begleitenden Objekte einschließt. Wenn wir einen Bonsai ziehen und ausstellen, müssen wir seine Höhe, Größe, Farbe, Beschaffenheit, Bewegung, sowie die Akzentpflanzen berücksichtigen. Wir müssen uns Gedanken über den Hintergrund machen, vor dem die Bäume ausgestellt werden, über die Ausstellungsfläche und dem Platz zwischen den Bäumen. Wenn man all diese Elemente gut verbindet, schafft man ein harmonisches Sein. Man kann keine Regeln aufstellen, um dies zu erreichen. Wir müssen die folgenden, voneinander abhängigen Basisgrundsätze berücksichtigen.

1 Hierarchie Man muß die Ordnung der verschiedenen Elemente wissen und verhindern, daß zwischen ihnen keine Konkurrenz aufkommt - Baum - Tisch - Akzentpflanze - Suiseki - andere Bäume.

Der Baum, als erster in der Hierarchie, beherrscht die anderen Elemente, die sich seiner Größe, Farbe und Bewegung unterordnen müssen. Auch die verschiedenen Teile des Baumes (Stamm, Äste, Blätter, Blüten) sind dieser hierarchischen Beziehung unterworfen und zwar nach Quantitätsfaktoren, wie beispielsweise Dicke und Länge aber was noch wichtiger ist, sie werden nach Qualitätsfaktoren, wie Proportionen, Farbe, Beschaffenheit und Form bestimmt.

Eine Hierarchie bedeutet nicht, daß einige Elemente weniger wichtig sind. Jedes Element kann eine entscheidende Rolle in der Komposition haben: Balance, Gegengewicht oder das Bild zu vervollständigen. Selbst ein kleiner Riß in der Hierarchieordnung kann auf die ganze Komposition wirken. Ein extremes Beispiel wäre, einer optisch schwere Schale für einen schlanken Baum zu wählen. Die Schale würde den Baum nicht ergänzen, da die Hierarchie nicht stimmt.

2 Maßstab Die Bonsaikunst ist nicht nur eine maßstabgerechte Reproduktion der Natur. Es ist eine symbolische Darstellung oder Abstraktion der Natur in Miniatur. Alle

al relationship between the tree (its own elements: branches roots, leaves, flowers) and its complementary elements (accent plants, suiseki, table) must work if the entity of the composition is to be believable. For example, trees with medium to large leaves (Fagus Sylvatica, Arbutus unedo) are more appropriate as bonsai of medium size or larger (50 - 100cm). For accent plants, we could use small-leaved ferns such as Ceterach officinarum Ac, rather than large-leaved species.

3 Harmony Another basic, although subjective impression where hierarchy and scale are complemented by tone and space between elements, austerity and sobriety in the use of materials. The proper relationship between all of these make a balanced, harmonious bonsai. All elements should have a natural link, being of similar origin. If we use trees from a cold climate with stones or accent plants from tropical zones, the harmony is destroyed – the feeling of naturalness is lost.

4 Function The first three points concern aesthetics and are spiritual, the rules are inspirational and cannot be found in books. All of them are governed by the function of the tree. We must know how to cultivate the tree, to direct its energy to achieve the desired image. Without this we can't develop sculptural, dynamic forms and the art of bonsai becomes impossible. Thus, to develop the art of bonsai one must first be proficient at cultivating trees. The growth, colour, leaf size and flowering of the tree all depend entirely on this ability.

di scala dell'intera opera. Questo rapporto proporzionale tra l'albero (ed i suoi elementi: rami, radici, foglie e fiori) ed i suoi elementi complementari (erbe di campagnia, suiseki, tavolo) devono funzionare affinchè l'entità della composizione possa essere credibile. Per esempio: alberi con foglie medie e grandi sono più appropriati come bonsai di taglia media ed oltre (50-100cm). Per gli 'accent plants', potremo utilizzare delle felci con le foglie piccole invece delle specie con le foglie grandi.

3 Armonia L'armonia è un'altra impressione basilare ma soggettiva dove gerarchia e scala vengono complementati dal tono e lo spazio tra gli elementi, austerità e sobrietà nell'utilizzo dei materiali. Il rapporto giusto tra tutti questi elementi risulta in un bonsai equilibrato ed armonioso. Tutti gli elementi dovrebbe avare un collegamento naturale, di origine simile. Se utilizziamo alberi provenienti da un clima freddo insieme a sassi o 'accent plants' da zone tropicali, l'armonia viene distrutta e la sensazione di naturalezza viene persa.

4 Funzione I primi tre punti riguardano l'estetica e sono spirituali, le regole sono ispiratrici e non possono essere travate nei libri. Tutti sono governati dalla funzione dell'albero. Noi dobbiamo sapere coltivare l'albero, e dirigere la sua energia per ottenere l'immagine desiderata. Senza tutto questo non possiamo sviluppare forme scolpite e dinamiche e l'arte del bonsai diventa impossibile. Pertanto per sviluppare l'arte del bonsai bisogna essere prima di tutto in grado di coltivare alberi. La crescita, il colore, dimensione delle foglie e fioritura dell'albero dipendono completamente da quest'abilità.

una reproducción a escala de la naturaleza, sino una representación simbólica a menor escala de la misma. Todo el conjunto debe funcionar a una escala proporcional. Una elección de plantas de acento con hoja mayor que la hoja del árbol, al que complementa, hace que se pierda la sensación de escala del conjunto. Esta relación proporcional entre el árbol y sus elementos (ramas, raíces, hojas, flores), y sus complementos (plantas de acento, suiseki, mesa expositora), debe funcionar para que la totalidad de la composición sea creíble. Por ejemplo, árboles con hoja medianas o grandes (Fagus sylvatica, Arbutus unedo), son más apropiadas para bonsais de tamaño medio o grande (50-100 cms). Para planta de acento, podremos utilizar helechos de hoja pequeña, como Ceterach officinarum Ac, en lugar de especies de hoja más grande.

3 Armonía Impresión subjetiva pero que es básica en aspectos como son los apuntados anteriormente: jerarquía y escala adecuada complementados por cromatismo, espacios entre los elementos, austeridad y sobriedad en el uso de los materiales. La adecuada relación entre todo hará que un bonsai armónico encuentre su punto de equilibrio. La naturalidad entre todos los elementos, esto es que la selección de materiales tenga un orígen igual o similar. Si utilizamos arboles de un clima frío con piedras o plantas de acento de un clima tropical, se destruye la armonía, el sentimiento de naturalidad se ha perdido.

4 Función Los trés puntos anteriores se refieren a aspectos estéticos que deberán seguir cánones, reglas y la inspiración e imaginación no escrita en manuales ni libros. Todos éstos principios están supeditados a que el árbol funcione. Debemos saber como cultivar el árbol, dirigir su energía para conseguir la imágen deseada. Sin ésto, no podemos desarrollar formas esculturales no dinámicas, y resulta imposible desarrollar el arte del bonsai, hay que ser previamente un buen cultivador, de ello dependen color, crecimiento, tamaño de hoja y floración del árbol.

tionner ensemble, à la même échelle. Si l'ont choisit des plantes «accent» avec des feuilles plus larges que celles de l'arbre qu'elles sont supposées complémenter, on détruit la bonne échelle de l'ensemble. Cette relation proportionnelle entre l'arbre (tous ses éléments: branches, racines, feuilles, fleurs) et ses éléments complémentaires (plantes «accent', suiseki, table) doivent marcher pour que l'entité de la composition soit crédible. Par exemple, les arbres qui ont des feuilles de taille moyenne ou large (Fagus sylvatica, Arbutus unedo) sont plus appropriés en tant que bonsaï de taille moyenne ou plus grande (50 -100cm). Pour les plantes «accent», on peut utiliser des fougères à petites feuilles comme Ceterach officinarum Ac, plutôt que des espèces à feuilles larges.

3 L'harmonie Un autre élément de base, bien que subjectif: la hiérarchie et l'échelle sont complementées par le ton et l'espace entre les éléments, l'austérité et la sobrieté dans l'utilisation des matériaux. Une bonne relation entre ces éléments donne un bonsaï équilibré et harmonieux. Tous les éléments doivent se joindre naturellement, car ils viennent de la même source. Si l'on utilise des arbres provenant de climats froids avec des roches et des plantes «accent» de zones tropicales, l'harmonie est détruite – l'impression de naturel est perdue.

4 La fonction Les 3 premiers points concernent l'esthétique et sont spirituels, les règles viennent de l'inspiration et ne peuvent être trouvées dans les livres. Tous sont gouvernés par la fonction de l'arbre. Il faut savoir comment cultiver l'arbre, diriger toute son énergie vers l'image désirée. Sans cela, on ne peut developper des formes sculpturales et dynamiques, l'art bonsaï devient impossible. Alors, pour développer l'art bonsaï, il faut d'abord savoir cultiver les arbres. La pousse, la couleur, la taille des feuilles et la floraison dépendent de ce savoir faire.

Elemente müssen im gleichen Maßstab miteinander funktionieren. Wenn man Akzentpflanzen auswählt, die Blätter haben, die größer sind als die Blätter des Baumes, den sie ergänzen sollen, wäre der ganze Eindruck von Maßstabstreue zerstört. Dieses Proportionsverhältnis zwischen dem Baum (seine eigenen Elemente: Äste, Wurzeln, Blätter, Blüten) und seinen ergänzenden Elemente (Akzentpflanzen, Suiseki, Tisch) muß eingehalten werden, wenn das Wesen der Komposition glaubhaft sein soll. Beispielsweise sind Bäume mit mittleren bis Großen Blättern (Fagus sylvatica, Arbutus unedo) für mittelgroße bis große Bonsai (50 - 100cm) besser geeignet. Als Akzentpflanze können wir anstelle von großblättrigen Arten lieber kleinblättrige Farne benutzen (z.B. Ceterach officinarum Ac).

3 Harmonie Ein anderer grundsätzlicher, wenn auch subjektiver Eindruck wenn Hierarchie und Maßstab von Klang und Raum zwischen den Elementen ergänzt werden ist die Einfachheit und Nüchternheit beim Gebrauch der Materialien. Das richtige Verhältnis zwischen all diesen Elementen, ergeben einen ausgewogenen, harmonischen Bonsai. Alle Elemente sollten ein natürliche Verbindung haben, sie sollten einen ähnlichen Ursprung aufweisen. Wenn wir Bäume aus einer kalten Klimazone mit Steinen oder Akzentpflanzen aus den Tropen zusammentun, ist die Harmonie zerstört - das Gefühl der Natürlichkeit ist velorengegangen.

4 Funktion Die drei ersten Punkte betreffen die Ästhetik und sind geistiger Natur, die Regeln unterliegen der Inspiration und stehen nicht in Büchern. Sie werden alle von der Funktion des Baumes regiert. Wir müssen wissen, wie wir den Baum kultivieren, wie wir seine Energie in die Bahnen lenken, um das gewünschte Bild zu erreichen. Ohne dies können wir keine skulpturellen, dynamischen Formen entwickeln und die Bonsaikunst wird unmöglich. Um also die Bonsaikunst zu entwickeln, muß man in der Kultivierung von Bäumen geübt sein. Die Größe, Farbe, Blattgröße und die Blüten des Baumes sind ganz von dieser Fähigkeit abhängig.

Propiedad del Museo Municipal de Alcobendas, Madrid

▲ **Fagus sylvatica**
⇕ 48cm
Yamadori 1987
⊏⊐ David Benavente, Kurama

Kevin Willson

Kevin Willson was born in 1959 in Essex, England. His appreciation for nature and love of art was apparent from an early age and by his late teens he had developed his talent as an artist. At the time he was greatly influenced by Japanese culture art. At this time he moved to the Kent countryside where he began to develop his horticultural skills through his involvement in the management of a large country estate.

The idea of bonsai was already in his mind and with his new horticultural knowledge, his eye for Japanese art and with the inspiration of the surrounding countryside, the seed for growing bonsai had been sown.

Kevin began to learn more about the art of bonsai by studying all the books available. Those which had the most affect on him were by Masahiko Kimura. He soon realised that yamadori material provided the natural qualities he preferred and spent most of his spare time walking the hills and searching disused chalk quarries for suitable material.

One of his first pieces of work, a formal upright Taxus baccata, collected in 1982, has won many Certificates of Special Merit and has been loaned to the British National Collection and exhibited at the Chelsea Flower Show. As time went by the material Kevin collected became more challenging and his own style of high mountain trees began to emerge.

Kevin has spent 5 years demonstrating at various national and society shows, along with many successful workshops throughout the UK. He enjoys sharing his knowledge of bonsai and has some dedicated students, many of whom are showing great potential.

Kevin Willson intends to continue sharing his knowledge of bonsai at home and abroad, while constantly creating high quality trees and improving his skills.

Kevin Willson è nato ad Essex, Inghilterra nel 1959. Fin da giovane aveva dimostrato una grande passione per la natura e l'arte, una sensibilità che in tarda adolescenza gli permise di sviluppare il suo talento di artista. Da allora fu molto influenzato dalla cultura artistica giapponese. Si trasferì nel Kent per approfondire le sue capacità orticolturali, prendendo in gestione una grande proprietà in campagna. L'idea del bonsai era già viva in lui ed insieme alle sue nuove conoscenze ortocolturali, il suo occhio per l'arte giapponese e l'ispirazione della campagna che lo circondava, cominciò ad appassionarsi a quest'arte

Kevin ha studiato tutti i libri disponibili per imparare sempre di più sull'arte del bonsai. Quelli che lo hanno ispirato principalmente sono stati scritti da Masahiko Kimura. Presto si accorse che il materiale yamadori forniva le caratteristiche che più stimolavano la sua creatività e pertanto passò molto del suo tempo libero cercando buoni materiali nelle cave abbandonate.

Ad una delle sue prime opere, un Taxus baccata in eretto formale raccolto nel 1982, furono assegnato molti premi per meriti speciali e fu prestato alla collezione nazionale britannica e mostrato alla Chelsea Flower Show. Col andare avanti del tempo il materiale che Kevin raccoglieva si presentava sempre più come una sfida, una sfida nella quale emerse il suo stile personale tipico degli alberi di alta montagna. Negli ultimi cinque anni Kevin si è esibito in varie mostre nazionali, nei Club, nonchè in molte dimostrazioni in Inghilterra che hanno riscosso un buon successo. Kevin ama molto condividere il suo sapere con altri bonsaisti, da anni si dedica all'insegnamento ed è circondato da allievi di grande capacità.

Kevin Willson intende continuare a condividere la sua conoscenza di bonsai sia nel suo paese che all'estero, mentre cerca di creare costantemente alberi di altissima qualità e di migliorare sempre le sue capacità.

▲ **Carpinus betulus**

Yamadori 1992

⬭ Derek Aspinall

◀ Taxus baccata

Yamadori 1982

Derek Aspin

Kevin Willson nació en 1959 en Essex, Inglaterra. Su aprecio por la naturaleza y su amor por el arte apareció desde una tierna edad y en su adolescencia avanzada desarrolló su talento de artista. Fué entonces muy influenciado por la cultura y el arte japonés y a su vez se transladó a la campiña de Kent, donde comenzó a desarrollar su habilidad en la horticultura a través de su papel como gerente de una gran mansión.

La idea de bonsai ya se albergaba en su mente y con su nuevo conocimiento horticultural, su ojo por el arte japonés y la inspiración de sus alrededores campestres, la semilla para el cultivo de bonsai, estaba sembrada.

Kevin comenzó a aprender más sobre el arte de bonsai mediante el estudio de todos los libros que estaban a su alcance. Los que más efecto surtieron en él, fueron los de Masahiko Kimura. Se dió cuenta rapidamente que el material yamadori proporcionaba las cualidades más deseables para su gusto, y dedicó la mayor parte de su tiempo libre paseando por las colinas y canteras en deshuso en busca de materiales apropiados.

Una de sus primeras piezas un Taxus baccata de forma recta y regular, recogido en 1982, ha sido premiado con muchos Certificados de Mérito y se ha prestado a la Colección Nacional Británica y expuesto en la Chelsea Flower Show. A medida que el tiempo transcurría el material coleccionado se volvió más complejo y su propio estilo de árboles de alta montaña comenzó a evolucionar.

Kevin ha estado dedicado durante cinco años a demostraciones en varios exhibiciones nacionales y sociales además de varios talleres de gran éxito a través del Reino Unido. Kevin disfruta compartiendo su conocimiento de bonsai y tiene varios estudiantes con mucha dedicación e interés, de los cuales un gran número destaca por su gran potencial. Kevin Willson procura continuar compartiendo su experiencia con bonsai en su país además de en el extranjero, mientras a su vez crea arboles de alta calidad y perfecciona su arte.

Kevin Willson est né en 1959 dans l'Essex, en Angleterre. Son appréciation de la nature et son amour de l'art sont évidents dès son plus jeune âge. Vers la fin de son adolescence, son talent artistique est déjà très développé. A cette période, il est très influencé par l'art dans la culture Japonaise. Il s'installe dans le Kent, à la campagne, où il gère une grande propriété et acquiert ainsi des compétences en horticulture. Il pensait déjà aux bonsaïs à cette époque. Avec ces nouvelles connaissances en horticulture, son œil pour l'art Japonais, et toute l' inspiration de la campagne environnante, le voilà prêt à faire pousser des bonsaïs.

Kevin commença à apprendre l'art des bonsaïs en étudiant tous les livres possibles. Ceux qui l'ont le plus influencé sont ceux de Masahiko Kimura. Il comprit vite que sa matière brute favorite était des arbres receuillis dans la nature. Ces arbres offraient toutes les qualités requises. Il commença donc à passer tout son temps libre à se promener dans la campagne à la recherche d'arbres dans les mines de craie désaffectées.

Une de ses premières pièces, un Taxus baccata de forme rigoureusement verticale, recueilli en 1982, a gagné plusieurs prix avec mention spéciale, a été prêté à la collection Nationale Britannique et exhibé au Chelsea Flower Show. Avec le temps, la matieère brute recueillie par Kevin devient de plus en plus stimulante et son propre style commence à apparaitre: un style d'arbres de haute montagne.

Kevin a passé 5 ans à faire des démonstrations et à mener des ateliers dans des clubs de bonsais et lors d' évènements nationaux à travers toute l' Angleterre. Il aime partager ses connaissances. Il a plusieurs étudiants sérieux dont certains ont beaucoup de talent.

Kevin Willson a l'intention de continuer à partager ses connaissances en Angleterre et à l'étranger, tout en continuant à créer des arbres de qualité et à perfectionner sa technique.

Kevin Willson wurde 1959 in Essex, England geboren. Seine Würdigung der Natur und seine Liebe zur Kunst war schon in jungen Jahren vorhanden und als Teenager entwickelte er sein Talent zum Künstler. Zu jener Zeit war er durch die japanische Kunstkultur sehr beeinflußt. Er zog auf das Land in der Graftschaft Kent, wo er anfing seine gärtnerische Fähigkeiten zu entwickeln, indem er zum Management eines großen Landguts gehörte.

Er hatte die Bonsaiidee schon im Kopf und mit seinem neuen gärtnerischen Wissen, seinem Auge für japanische Kunst und durch die Inspiration der Landschaft in der Umgebung war die Idee, Bonsai geboren. Kevin lernte mehr über die Bonsaikunst, indem er alle verfügbaren Bücher studierte. Die größte Wirkung hatten Masahiko Kimuras Bücher auf ihn. Schnell merkte er, daß Yamadoris die natürlichen Qualitäten aufzeigten, die er bevorzugte. So verbrachte er die meiste Freizeit damit, in den Hügeln herumzulaufen und in stillgelegten Kreidesteinbrüchen nach geeignetem Material zu suchen. Eine seiner ersten Arbeiten, ein streng aufrechter Taxus baccata, den er 1982 gesammelt hatte, wurde mehrfach ausgezeichnet und als Leihgabe der 'Britisch National Collection' zur Verfügung gestellt. Außerdem wurde er bei der 'Chelsea Flower Show' ausgestellt. Mit der Zeit wurde das Material, das Kevin sammelte immer herausfordernder und sein eigener Stil von Hochgebirgsbäumen trat in Erscheinung.

Kevin hat fünf Jahre damit verbracht, Demonstrationen auf zahlreichen nationalen und lokalen Ausstellungen zu geben. Außerdem hat er gleichzeitig in ganz England erfolgreiche Workshops durchgeführt. Er hat Freude daran, sein Wissen über Bonsai mit anderen zu teilen. Einige seiner ergebenen Schüler zeigen ein großes Potential. Kevin Willson beabsichtigt weiterhin sein Bonsaiwissen mit anderen zu Hause und im Ausland zu teilen, während er laufend Bäume von hoher Qualität gestaltet und seine Fähigkeiten verfeinert.

Yamadori Bonsai

Kevin Willson

Yamadori Bonsai, 2 Hill Cottgae, Hog Hill, Bearsted, Maidstone, Kent ME14 4JX, UK
Tel: 0044 (0)1622 736802

Kevin Willson

THE MOST ENGLISH OF TREES

The main problem with obtaining yamadori material is finding it. The right type of tree occurs rarely in nature. It takes many hours of hiking, studying geological maps and gaining permission to acquire the best material. Areas where the environment is extreme, such as coastal areas with their strong sea gales, quarries of slate, chalk or granite, and exposed mountainous regions are he best locations. Excellent yamadori can also be found where animals are allowed to graze.

Yew are difficult to find as they only grow wild in small sections along the length of England, mainly on chalk uplands.

The yew has a very strong history in England. In the middle-ages every village had to grow its quota of yew wood for longbows. Some people describe the yew as 'the graveyard tree'. One theory is that these ancient yew trees survive in church yards is that either they were planted there to protect them from grazing animals in order to meet the 'bow quota'. Another is that, if the tree is very ancient and on the north side of the church, it was almost certainly a druid worship site. When Christianity spread to southern England, churches were built next to the pagan worship sites to help convert the Druids.

I choose yew because of its remarkable tolerance to sculpting techniques. Many trees have wood with no longevity in exposed areas. On the other hand, yew is extremely durable and retains its virtue indefinitely when carved. When King Henry VIII's flagship, 'The Mary Rose', was raised from the sea bed after 440 years, 38 long bows were discovered in such good condition that archaeologists were able to re-string some of them.

The Yew also has fantastic, deep coral bark and the contrast of the sculpted areas against the rich green foliage is incredible. The image that I am personally trying to create is that of trees of great antiquity, with their hollow interiors and branches

L'ALBERO PIU INGLESE CHE C'E

La difficoltà di ottenere materiale yamadori è nel cercarlo. Esiste raramente in natura l'albero perfetto. Ci vogliono molte ore di cammino, studiare carte geologiche e bisogna richiedere dei permessi per acquisire il materiale migliore. Luoghi dove l'ambiente è estremo, per esempio lungo la costa dove soffiano forti venti dal mare, cave d'ardesia, gesso o granite, e regioni montagnose esposte agli elementi sono i luoghi ideali. Si possono trovare Yamadori anche nei luoghi dove pascolano gli animali.

Il tasso è un essenza difficile da trovare in quanto cresce in natura soltanto in piccole zone lungo l'Inghilterra, principalmente sui alti-piani gessosi. Il tasso ha una grandissima tradizione in Inghilterra. Nel medioevo ogni villaggio era tenuto a coltivare la sua quota di legno di tasso per gli la costruzione degli archi. Certe persone descrivono il tasso come 'albero da cimitero'.

Esiste una leggenda che parla di questi tassi vecchissimi che crescono nei cimiteri. Essi venivano impiegati per proteggere questi luoghi sacri dagli animali che pascolavano permettendogli quindi di raggiungere le dimensioni sufficenti per realizzare degli archi. Un'altra leggenda racconta che, se l'albero è molto vecchio e situato al lato nord della chiesa, allora quel luogo è stato un sito rituale dei druidi. Quando il cristianesimo si stava diffondendo nel sud dell'Inghilterra, furono costruiti delle chiese accanto ai siti di preghiera pagani per tentare di convertire i druidi.

Ho scelto il tasso perchè si presta facilmente alla creazione di Jin e Shari. Tanti alberi possiedono un legno senza longevità, ma il tasso è estremamente resistente e mantiene le sue virtù indefinitivamente quando viene scolpito. Quando la nave di Enrico VIII 'The Mary Rose' fu recuperata dal fondo del mare dopo 440 anni, furono scoperti 38 archi in un condizione tale da permettere ai archeologi di riutilizzarli ancora.

EL ARBOL INGLÉS POR EXELENCIA

El problema principal para obtener material yamadori es simplemente el encontrarlo. El tipo de árbol idóneo se halla raramente en la naturaleza. Consume muchas horas caminando, estudiando mapas geológicos y adquiriendo permiso para la obtención del material deseado. Areas donde el medio es extremo, como lugares costeros con sus feroces galernas, canteras de pizarra, calcita o granito, y regiones montañosas son los lugares propicios. Excelente yamadori también puede ser hallado en zonas donde predominen animales de pasto.

Los tejos son muy difíciles de encontrar, ya que solamente crecen salvajes en secciones muy pequeñas dispersas por toda Inglaterra especialmente en meseta de suelo calizo. El tejo ha tenido una historia muy importante en Inglaterra. En la edad media todos los pueblos tenian la obligación de cultivar una debida cuota de bosque de tejos para la producción de arcos. Algunas personas conocen el tejo como 'el árbol de los cementerios'.

Una teoria dice que estos arboles fueron plantados en cementerios para ser protegidos de animales de pasto, de esta manera cumplian con el número reglamentario de arboles. Otra teoría dice que cuando el árbol es muy antiguo, y está en la parte norte de la iglesia, es casi seguro que ese era un lugar para rituales drúidas. Cuando la cristiandad se difundió por el sur de Inglaterra, las iglesias eran construidas contiguas a un lugar de veneracion pagána con el objeto de convertirles en cristianos.

Yo elegí el tejo debido a su gran tolerancia a las diversas técnicas de escultura. Hay un gran número de arboles cuya madera carece de longevidad en las partes expuestas. Por otro lado, el tejo es extremadamente durable y retiene su calidad aún siendo tallado. Cuando el buque escuadra de Enrique VIII 'The Mary Rose' fue sacado a flote 440 años más tarde, treinta y ocho arcos fueron descubiertos en tal óptima condición, que los arqueólogos fueron capaces de poner a algunos de ellos, cuerdas nuevas.

LE PLUS ANGLAIS DE TOUS LES ARBRES

Le plus dur avec les yamadori, c'est qu'il faut les trouver! Les arbres idéaux sont rares dans la nature. Pour acquérir la matière première idéale, il faut passer de longues heures à marcher, à étudier des cartes géologiques et à obtenir les permissions nécessaires pour déterrer les arbres. Les meilleurs endroits sont ceux où l'environnement est extrême, comme les côtes aux bord de la mer, là où il y a du vent, les mines d'ardoise, de craie, de granite, et les régions montagneuses exposées. De beaux Yamadori se trouvent aussi là où les herbivores broutent.

Les ifs sont difficiles à trouver parce qu'ils ne poussent que dans certains endroits en Angleterre, surtout sur les plateaux au sol crayeux.

L' if est étroitement lié à l'histoire de l'Angleterre. Au Moyen Age, tous les villages devaient faire pousser un certain nombre d'ifs pour faire des arcs. Certaines personnes le decrivent comme l'arbre des cimetières. Une théorie suggère que ces ifs étaient plantés dans les jardins des églises pour les protéger des animaux au temps où l'on avait besoin de leur bois pour les arcs. Ils y survivent depuis le moyen age. Une autre théorie énonce que si l'arbre est très vieux et qu'il est planté du côte nord de l'église, c'était sûrement un site de rites druides. Quand le christianisme s'est répandu jusqu'au sud de l'Angleterre, les églises furent construites à côté des sites paiens pour essayer de reconvertir les druides.

J'ai choisi l'if parcequ'il tolère remarquablement bien les techniques de sculpture. Beaucoup d'arbres ont un bois qui ne résiste pas bien aux intempéries. L'if, très résistant, conserve cette vertu même quand il est sculpté. Quand l'épave du bateau d'Henry VIII «La Marie Rose» fut sortie de la mer 440 ans après son naufrage, 38 arcs d'if furent découverts en tellement bon état que les archéologues purent les retendre avec des cordes.

L'if a aussi une écorce fantastique,

DER 'ENGLISCHSTE' ALLER BÄUME

Das Hauptproblem Yamadorimaterial zu bekommen, ist, dieses zu finden. Der richtige Typ von Baum kommt in der Natur selten vor. Man muß viele Stunden wandern, geologische Karten studieren und die Erlaubnis zum Ausgraben einholen, um das beste Material zu erlangen. Die besten Fundorete sind da, wo die Gebiete extreme Umweltbedingungen haben, wie beispielsweise Küstengebiete mit ihren starken Stürmen, Schiefer - Kreide - oder Granitsteinbrüche oder Bergregionen in exponierter Lage.

Excellente Yamadori kann man auch dort finden, wo Tiere weiden dürfen. Eiben sind nicht leicht zu finden, da sie in der freien Natur nur in bestimmten kleinen Abschnitten vorkommen, die sich in England von Nord nach Süd im Oberland auf Kreidefelsen befinden. Die Eibe hat in England eine ausgeprägte Geschichte. Im Mittelalter mußte jedes Doref eine bestimmte Anzahl von Eiben für Langbögen anpflanzen. Einige Leute bezeichnen die Eibe auch als 'Kirchhofbaum'. Eine Theorie, warum diese uralten Eiben in Kirchhöfen überlegen, ist, daß sie dort gepflanzt wurden, um vor weiden Tieren geschützt zu sein, damit die 'Bogenquote' erreicht wurde. Eine andere Theorie besagt, daß wenn der uralte Baum an der Nordseite der Kirche steht, er wahrscheinlich eine Kultstätte der Druiden war.

Als sich das Christentum nach Südengland ausbreitete, baute man die Kirchen in die Nähe der heidnischen Kultstätten um die Druiden leichter zu konvertieren. Ich habe Eigen deswegen ausgewählt, weil sie eine bemerkenswerte Toleranz in Hinblick auf Gestaltungstechniken habeb. Das Holz vieler Bäume ist in exponierten Gebergen nicht langlebig. Eiben haven jedoch eine hohe Lebensdauer und behalten ihre Gestalt, wenn die bearbeitet sind, für unbegrenzte Zeit.

Als das Flaggschiff König Henry des Achten, die 'Mary Rose' nach 440 Jahren vom Meeresboden ans Tageslicht gehievt wurde, waren 38 Langbögen in solch guter Verfassung, daß Archäologen einigen davon wieder Spannkraft verleihen konnten. Die Eibe hat

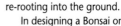

re-rooting into the ground.

In designing a Bonsai one needs to tell the story of the tree. If the story does not make sense then your final design will have no meaning. We have all seen examples of this. A tree in nature is struck by lightning, was it struck 100, 50, or 30 years ago? The movement of time and the elements will work more profoundly over the passing years.

Also when designing any bonsai one must look for a powerful buttress or 'nebari'. If the tree looks as if it is grasping the earth then the image is set for the rest of the tree.

With yamadori, the elements have already worked their magic on the tree so you will have to work with what the tree has to offer. This takes enormous sensitivity to the trees naturalness. If you study the ancient trees in the wild you will see the branches undulating and snaking.

To get a totally crisp image it is necessary to wire every branch, sub-branch, twig and shoot. Only by constant wiring and re-wiring will you obtain a totally natural end product.

I personally have been deeply inspired by the works of Masahiko Kimura and have also had great encouragement from many top English Bonsai artists such as Peter Adams, Dan Barton, Colin Lewis and Bill Jordan.

Many people believe bonsai to be a hobby, if it is done with the full passion that is necessary I believe it becomes a way of life. You never reach the end with yamadori – there is always that 'perfect' tree out there that you are constantly trying to find

Il tasso possiede anche una corteccia di un bellissimo colore corallo scuro ed il contrasto tra le parti scolpite e la chioma verde è incredibile. L'immagine che sto cercando di creare è quella di alberi di grande antichità con i tronchi vuoti e i rami che si radicano nella terra.

Quando si progetta un bonsai bisogna raccontare la sua storia. Se la storia non ha un senso anche il tuo progetto non ne avrà uno. Abbiamo tutti visto esempi del genere. In natura ci sono alberi che sono stati colpiti dal fulmine 30, 50 100 anni fa e con il trascorrere del tempo, gli elementi, continuano sempre a infierire.

Un'altro fattore da considerare quando si progetta un bonsai è quello di cercare una potente contrafforte o 'nebari'. Se l'albero sembra aggrapparsi alla terra allora l'immagine viene resa stabile per la parte restante dell'albero. Nelle piante raccolte in natura, gli elementi hanno già fatto magia sull'albero pertanto bisogna lavorare con ciò che offre l'albero. Per questo ci vuole una sensibilità enorme per la naturalezza dell'albero. Se studiate alberi vecchi in natura vedrete i rami ondulati e serpeggianti.

Per ottenere un'immagine perfettamente limpida bisogna applicare del filo ad ogni ramo, sotto-ramo, ramoscello e germoglio. E' soltanto tramite questa procedura di legatura con filo e rilegatura che si ottiene un prodotto finale completamente naturale.

Sono stato personalmente molto colpito dal lavoro di Masahiko Kimura e ho avuto molto incorraggiamento da tanti esperti ed artisti di bonsai inglese, quali Peter Adams, Dan Barton, Colin Lewis e Bill Jordan.

Molti credono che il bonsai sia soltanto un hobby, mentre credo che se viene affrontato con una passione completa diventa un modo di vivere. Raccogliere piante in natura è un piacere che non avrà mai fine, là fuori ci sarà sempre l'albero perfetto che ti aspetta.

El tejo tiene asímismo una corteza de un magnífico color oscuro. Que al ser contrastado con las áreas esculpidas y el follaje de un verde fuerte, es increible. La imagen que yo, personalmente trato de crear, es la de arboles de una gran antigüedad, con sus entrañas huecas y sus ramas hechando raices en el suelo. Al diseñar un Bonsai, se necesita contar la historia de ese árbol. Si la historia no tiene una lógica el diseño final por lo tanto no tendrá sentido. Todos nosotros hemos visto alguna vez un caso así. Un árbol en la naturaleza que ha sido golpeado por un rayo, ¿fué herido hace 100, 50, 30 años? El movimiento del tiempo y de los elementos dejarán una huella más profunda a medida que pasan los años.

Por otro lado cuando se diseña un bonsai, se debe buscar un apoyo poderoso o nebari. Si el árbol da la impresión de aferrarse fuertemente a la tierra esa será consiguientemente la imagen completa del árbol.

Con yamadori, los elementos ya han dado su toque mágico a la planta por lo tanto tendrémos que trabajar con lo que el árbol nos ofrece de por sí. Esto proporciona una gran sensibilidad en el bonsai que a su vez contribuye a su naturalidad.

Si estudiamos lo arboles centenarios silvestres podremos ver las diversas contorsiones de las ramas ondulándose y serpenteándose. Para conseguir una imagen vigorosa es necesario el alambrado de todas las ramas, ramillas y brotes. Sólo con constante alambrado y realambrado conseguiremos obtener un producto final de aspecto totalmente natural.

Yo personalmente he sido profundamente inspirado por el trabajo de Masahiko Kimura y asímismo he sido alentado por muchos grandes artistas ingleses como Peter Adams, Dan Barton, Colin Lewis y Bill Jordan.

Mucha gente consideran el bonsai como un pasatiempo, si se practica con pasión absoluta, cosa que es necesaria, se convierte en un estilo de vida. Nunca conseguiremos alcanzar el final con el yamadori – siempre existirá ese árbol 'perfecto' en algún lugar, que constantemente tratamos de encontrar.

d'une couleur corail. Les parties sculptées forment un contraste incroyable avec le feuillage vert foncé. L'image que j'essaye de créer est celle d'un arbre très vieux avec un tronc creux et des branches qui se replantent dans le sol.

Quand on stylise un bonsaï, il faut raconter l'histoire de l'arbre. Si l'histoire n'a aucum sens, alors la forme finale n'en aura pas non plus. Nous avons tous vu de tels exemples. La foudre tombe sur un arbre. Est ce que ça s'est passé il y a 100, 50 ou 30 ans? L'effet du temps et des éléments travaille plus profondement chaque année.

Quand on stylise un bonsaï, il faut aussi essayer de créer un contrefort puissant, ou des racines visibles. Si l'arbre a l'air de s'accrocher au sol, alors, ceci forme un image décisive pour le reste de l'arbre. Avec les yamadori, les éléments naturels ont déjà sculpté l'arbre. Il faut utiliser ce que l'arbre a à offrir. Ceci demande une grande sensibilité envers les qualités naturelles de l'arbre. Quand on étudie un très vieil arbre dans la nature, on voit les branches onduler, serpenter.

Pour obtenir une image claire, il est nécessaire de ligaturer toutes les branches, tous les rameaux, tous les bourgeons. C'est seulement en ligaturant et en religaturant constamment qu'on obtiendra un fini naturel.

Le travail de Masahiko Kimura a été, et est encore pour moi, une profonde source d' inspiration. J'ai aussi reçu beaucoup d'encouragements de la part de plusieurs grands artistes de bonsaï Anglais comme Peter Adams, Dan Barton, Colin Lewis et Bill Jordan.

Beaucoup de gens croient que créer un bonsaï est juste un passe temps. Pour moi, si c'est fait avec la passion nécessaire, c'est plutôt un mode de vie. On n'atteint jamais la perfection avec un yamadori. Il y a toujours cet arbre parfait qui nous échappe.

außerdem eine tiefkorallenrote Rinde und der Kontrast zwischen den gejinnten Partien und den dunkelgrünen Nadeln ist unglaublich. Das Bild, das ich persönlich erschaffen möchte, ist das von uralten Bäumen, die mit ihrem hohlen Inneren und holen Ästen sich wieder in die Erde einwurzeln.

Wenn man einen Bonsai gestaltet, muß man die Geschichte des Baumes erzählen. Wenn die Geschichte keinen Sinn ergibt, hat Ihre endgültige Gestaltung keine Bedeutung. Wir alle haben solche Beispiele schon gesehen. Ein Baum in der Natur wird durch einen Blitz getroffen. War es vor 100, 50 oder vor 30 Jahren? Auch die Zeit und die Elemente werden über die Jahre gründlich zum Aussehen des Baumes beitragen.

Wenn man irgend einen Bonsai gestalten will, muß man auf einen starken Wurzelansatz oder 'Nebari' achten. Sieht der Baum aus als ob er in die Erde hineingreift, ist das Bild für den ganzen Baum festgelegt. Bei Yamadori haben die Element bereits ihren Zauber auf den Baum ausgeübt, und Sie müssen mit dem arbeiten, was der Baum bietet. Es fordert viel Sensitivität für die Natürlichkeit des Baumes. Wenn Sie die uralten Bäume in der Natur studieren, werden Sie bemerken, daß sich die Äste schlängeln und Wellen werfen.

Um ein völlig lebhafte Darstellung zu bekommen, muß man jeden Ast, jede Verästelung, jeden Zweig und jeden Sproß drahten. Nur durch andauerndes Drahten und Entdrahten erzielen Sie ein völlig natürliches Endprodukt. Ich persönlich wurde tief durch die Werke Masahiko Kimuras inspiriert. Auch die großen englischen Bonsaikünstler wie Peter Adams, Dan Barton, Colin Lewis und Bill Jordan haben mich sehr unterstützt.

Viele Leute glauben, daß Bonsai ein Hobby sei. Wenn man es jedoch mit der ganzen Leidenschaft die nötig ist, betreibt, wird es eine Lebenseinstellung. Mit Yamadori erreichen Sie nie ein Ende – es gibt immer 'den' perfekten Baum irgendwo da drauen, den Sie immer zu finden suchen.

Taxus baccata

Yamadori 1984

Derek Aspinall

▲ **Taxus baccata**

Yamadori 1990

⬭ Tokoname

The European Bonsai Association

Malcolm Hughes, President, European Bonsai Association

During the 20th century, the world has experienced some of the most significant changes ever. In the midst of these, advancements in travel and communication have opened a vast new range of opportunities and experiences to millions of people, including the art of bonsai.

Since the 1970s, an ever-increasing number of bonsai societies has been established in every European country. Initially, these societies functioned in isolation, dependent on a handful of knowledgeable individuals and a limited range of books. The need to establish effective links between societies and nations became obvious and soon a number of countries set up their own national organisations.

In 1982, at the invitation of Paul Lesniewicz, representatives of bonsai clubs from Belgium, France, Italy, Germany, Luxembourg, Spain, Switzerland and the United Kingdom came together at the 1st European Bonsai Convention, Heidelberg, where discussions took place about the formation of a European association. Later the same year, at the 1st Congres of the Asoción Española de Bonsai, delegates discussed draft bye-laws.

In September 1984, the European Bonsai Association (EBA) was born. Since then, EBA has strengthened its membership and has forged links between the member countries. One of the most effective means being the annual conventions, hosted by a different country each year. Here enthusiasts have the opportunity to see first hand the best examples of European bonsai. Whilst many do not share a common language or culture, the common interest in bonsai has proved an intriguing means of establishing new friendships. Through the efforts of individuals and clubs within Europe, the current trends will hopefully continue well into the next century.

Durante il XXº secolo, il mondo ha subito alcuni dei più importanti cambiamenti nella storia. Uno degli interessi che si è diffuso più rapidamente è appunto il bonsai.

Dagli anni settanta, un sempre più crescente numero di associazioni bonsai sono stati fondate in quasi tutti i paesi Europei, insieme a molti punti vendita. Inizialmente, tante delle associazioni operavano in isolamento e si affidavano a poche persone con una conoscenza bonsaistica ed un numero limitato di libri specializzati. La necessità di stabilire relazioni tra associazioni e paesi divenne fondamentale e presto alcuni paesi Europei fondarono le loro organizzazioni nazionali.

Nel 1982 alcuni reppresentanti dei club bonsai provenienti dal Belgio, Francia, Italia, Germania, Lussemburgo, Spagna, Svizzera ed dal Regno Unito, furono invitati da Paul Lesniewicz al raduno del primo European Bonsai Convention a Heidelberg. Durante questo evento, si discusse riguardo la formazione di un'associazione Europea di bonsai. Ci furono ulteriori progressi nello stesso anno al primo congresso dell'Associazione Spagnola del Bonsai, dove gli invitati discussero la proposta dello statuto.

Pertanto nel 1984, nacque l'European Bonsai Association (EBA). Da allora, l'EBA ha visto un grande aumento dei soci e ha allacciato dei collegamenti tra i paesi soci tramite un metodo efficace di convenzioni annuali, gestiti da un paese diverso ogni anno. Come forma artistica orticulturale, questi eventi fornendo l'opportunità di vedere di prima mano i migliori esempi di bonsai Europei. Mentre tanti non condividono una comune lingua o cultura, gli interessi comuni per il bonsai sono un interessante modo per stabilire nuove amicizie. Attraverso gli sforzi di individuali e clubs europei si spera che le attuali tendenze continuino nel prossimo secolo ed oltre.

E

Durante el siglo veinte, el mundo ha experimentado algunos de los cambios más significativos en el curso de la historia. En medio de estos cambios, los avances en el transporte y la comunicación, han abierto una vasta gama de oportunidades y experiencias para millones de personas. Uno de estos intereses ha sido el arte de bonsai.

Desde la década de los setenta un número en ascenso de sociedades de bonsai se han establecido en casi todos los paises europeos. En un principio la mayoria de las sociedades funcionaban aisladas, dependiendo en gran parte de un grupo de individuos con conocimiento en este campo y un número limitado de libros. La necesidad de establecer vínculos efectivos entre las diversas sociedades y paises era patente y rápidamente algunos paises europeos emprendieron en sus propias organizaciones nacionales.

En 1982 en la invitación de Paul Lesniewicz, representantes de clubs de bonsai de Bélgica, Francia, Italia Luxemburgo, España, Suiza y Gran Bretaña se reunieron en la primera Convención Europea de Bonsai sostenida en Heilderberg. En esta convención se realizaron discursiones informales sobre la formación de una asociación europea de bonsai. Más tarde ese mismo año en el Congreso de La Asociación Española de Bonsai, los representantes discutieron los anteproyectos de leyes.

Fue así como la Asociación Europea de Bonsai (EBA) surgió. Desde entonces EBA ha ganado fuerza en el número de miembros y ha tramado una estrecha relación con los demás paises asociados. Uno de los procedimientos más efectivos son las convenciones mantenidas anualmente, dirigidas por un grupo diferente cada año. Aunque muchos sean los que no comparten una lengua o cultura en común, el interés compartido por bonsai ha demostrado ser una forma poco usual de forjar nuevos lazos de amistad. Mediante los esfuerzos de algunos individuos y los diferentes clubs europeos, es presumible que esta oleada de entusiastas continue el próximo siglo e incluso más allá.

 F

Durant le vingtième siècle, le monde a connu les changements politiques et sociaux les plus importants de toute l'histoire. A travers ces changements, les progrès dans les voyages et la communication ont ouvert à des millions de gens de nouvelles perspectives, de nouvelles expériences. Il y a moins d'un siècle, de telles expériences n'étaient accessibles qu'à quelques privilégiés. L'un de ces passe-temps s'est répandu rapidement: l'art du bonsaï.

Depuis les années soixante dix, un nombre toujours croissant de sociétés de bonsaï et des pépinières spécialisées se sont établies dans pratiquement tous les pays d'Europe. Au depart, ces sociétés étaient isolées et dependaient de quelques personnes qui possèdaient une connaissance des bonsaïs et une collection limitée de livres sur le sujet. Le besoin d'établir des liens entre les sociétés et les pays devint vite évident et bientôt, un certain nombre de pays Européens fondèrent leur propre organisation nationale.

En 1982, à l'invitation de Paul Lesniewicz, les représenter de clubs de bonsaï de Belgique, de France, d'Italie, d'Allemagne, du Luxembourg, d'Espagne, de Suisse et de Grande Bretagne se réunirent à Heidelberg, à la première convention Européenne de bonsaï. Lors de cet évènement, des discussions concernant la formation d'une association Européenne eurent lieu. Des progrès apparurent tard dans la même année au premier congrès de l'Asocicion Española de Bonsaï, où les délégués discutèrent les propositions de législation.

C'est ainsi qu'en septembre 1984 est née l'Association Européenne de Bonsaï (EBA). Depuis, le nombre de membres de l'EBA a augmenté et des liens se sont tissés entre les pays membres. Pour cela, les conventions annuelles sont très utiles; elle sont organisées par un pays d'accueil différent chaque année. Celles-ci rendent l'art horticole bonsaï plus accessible aux amateurs. Des experts venus du monde entier y sont invités et c'est l'occasion de voir les meilleurs exemples de bonsaïs Européens. Bien que beaucoup ne partagent pas la même langue ni la même culture, l'attrait pour les bonsaïs est une façon fascinante d'établir de nouvelles amitiés. Grâce aux efforts d'individus et de clubs à travers l'Europe, souhaitons que cette tendance continue dans le siecle avenir et même au-dela.

D

Im 20. Jahrhundert hat die Welt einige ihrer wichtigsten Veränderungen im Lauf ihrer Geschichte erlebt. Inmitten dieser Veränderungen haben Fortschritte beim Reisen und bei der Kommunikation Millionen von Leuten neue, umfassende Möglichkeiten und Erfahrungen eröffnet. Ein solches Interesse, das sich sehr schnell ausgebreitet hat, ist die Bonsaikunst.

Seit den 70er Jahren haben sich in fast jedem europäischen Land Bonsai - Vereinigungen etabliert und auch spezielle Baumschulen. Zuerst waren viele Vereinigungen nur isoliert tätig und waren von einer Handvoll Individualisten abhängig, die etwas über Bonsai wußten und eine begrenzte Anzahl von Fachbüchern hatten. Der Bedarf, effektive Verbindungen zu anderen Vereinigungen und Ländern zu schaffen wurden offenbar und bald richteten einige europäische Länder ihre nationalen Organisationen ein.

1982 kamen auf Einladung von Paul Lesniewicz Vertreter der Bonsaiclubs von Belgien, Frankreich, Italien, Deutschland, Luxembourg, Spanien der Schweiz und Großbritanniens zum 1. Europäischen Bonsaikongreß in Heidelberg zusammen. Bei diesem Anlaß wurden nicht formelle, erste Diskussionen über die Gründung einer europäischen Bonsaivereinigung geführt. Im gleichen Jahr, etwas später, wurden beim 1. Kongreß der Asocicion Espanola, von der Delegierten die vorgeschlagenen Statuten diskutiert.

So wurde im September 1984 die European Bonsai Association (EBA) aus der Taufe gehoben. Seitdem hat die EBA ihre Mitgliedschaft gestärkt und hat Verbindungen zwischen den Mitgliedsländern geschmiedet. Eines der effektivsten Mittel sind die jährlichen Kongresse, die jedes Jahr von einem anderen Land ausgerichtet werden.

Bonsai erzeugt ganz klar ein Instrument, das Menschen verschiedener Länder und mit verschiedenen Werdegängen zusammenbringt. Während viele keine gemeinsame Sprache oder Kultur teilen, hat das allgemeine Interesse an Bonsai als Neugier erregendes Mittel bestätigt, welches auch neue Freundschaften erzeugt. Durch die Anstrengungen die Einzelne und acuh Clubs innerhalb Europas machen, hofft man, daß die gegenwärtigen Trends in das nächste Jahrhundert und darüberhinaus, weitergehen.

European Bonsai Association
Heliotropenlaan 3
B-1030 Brussels
Belgium

欧州盆栽

　１８７８年のパリ万国博覧会、ついで１９０９年のロンドン万国博覧会にて大衆に紹介されて以来、盆栽は徐々にヨーロッパにおいて市民権を得てきた。盆栽愛好家が急速に増えてきたのは１９７０年の日本万国博覧会からのことである。盆栽とひと口に言っても、ヨーロッパのそれは中国を含める東南アジア系のものと日本の盆栽との二つがあり、前者は主に室内用盆栽として、日本の盆栽は屋外用のものとしてあつかわれている。そして、ヨーロッパにおける室内用盆栽が市場の９０パーセントを占めている所に注目したい。つまり、樹木を育てる立場にたった盆栽愛好よりも、観賞園芸としてのあつかわれ方が今もって多いと云うことである。

　ヨーロッパ人が本格的な愛好家として盆栽を始める動機には多種多様なものがある。園芸のひとつとして始める人、盆栽の創作性に惹かれて手がける人、東洋文化嗜好の表れとして愛好する人、仏教思想を背景にして模索する人、等々、極めて幅広い。長年盆栽を愛育している人の中には、盆栽が、自然木の縮図化された単なるコピーではなく、わび、さび、幽玄などの日本的美意識の表現、しかも大自然とその一部にすぎない人間との調和を、自己の感性をおりこみながら、樹木を媒体にして盆上に表現すると云う日本盆栽の究極を深く感じとっている人も少なくない。

　盆栽が、自然を対象とした単なる個人的表現の技術にすぎないものであったとすれば、これほど世界中に愛好者を生んではいなかったであろうと思われる。人種を越えた、人間全般に共鳴させる詩的な要素が盆栽にはあるようだ。

　ヨーロッパにおける盆栽の特色はその創作性にあると云って良い。ほとんどの愛好家が、実生あるいは山取りによって荒木から自力のみで「ボンサイ」を作ろうとする。手本となるものは日本―中国の数少い盆栽写真のみである。盆栽用種木の生産者がほとんど皆無に近いことや、輸入物が高価であると云う事も原因している。この様な条件下で作られた盆栽に日本では見られない独創的な樹型が多いことは容易に理解できることである。また、気候、地形、あるいは樹種の違いも日本の盆栽とは一風異った作風をみせる因となっている。ヨーロッパのブナの木では日本の白肌のブナの表現は出せない。西洋の樫は鬱蒼としてどこまでも力強い。種としての樹が持つ性質あるいは表現が盆栽を創作する上で大切なことは洋の東西を問わず変らない。そこから出来てくる樹型の違いは盆栽技術云々とは関係なく、必然的なものである。この辺にも多国籍化する「盆栽」の可能性が秘められていると思う。

　数百年前、中国から渡ってきた盆景が日本人の感性をもって同化され今日の盆栽が生まれたように、世界各国の盆栽は、日本盆栽の思想を踏まえた上で今後とも独自の発展を遂げてゆくであろうし、そのような発展を目指してこそ初めて、純粋な万国共通性を持ったひとつの芸術と成り得ると思う。

　このヨーロッパ人によって創作された盆栽の作品集が何らかの形で日本の盆栽家各位の参考に供されるならば多大な幸と云うべきである。

フランス語盆栽誌「盆栽家」主筆、　大沼　康

F.BLOCH

ファラン・ブロック
　　　　　　（オランダ）

１９６５年オランダに生まれる。
１９９２年に渡日し大宮にて盆栽
を学ぶ。１９９３年以降盆栽を職
業とし欧米各国で盆栽を教える。
日本の盆栽を基点に独自の作風を
模索するアーティストのひとり。

P.7
樹種：　一位
樹高：　７０cm
樹齢：　１６５年
原産：　日本
鉢：　　ヴァルサル　スタジオ

P.8
樹種：　チャボヒバ
樹高：　６０cm
樹齢：　３５年
原産：　オランダ
鉢：　　常滑

P.14
樹種：　黒松
樹高：　８０cm
樹齢：　７０年
原産：　日本
鉢：　　常滑

P.15
樹種：　糸杉
樹高：　６０cm
樹齢：　７０年
原産：　イタリア
鉢：　　ジョン・ダウソン

P.16
樹種：　五葉松
樹高：　６５cm
樹齢：　２３年
原産：　日本
鉢：　　カネコ

P.17
樹種：　五葉松
樹高：　４５cm
樹齢：　２３年
原産：　日本
鉢：　　ファランド・ブロック

P.FERMANI

パトリジオ・フェルマニ
　　　　　　（イタリア）

１９７０年代より盆栽に興味をも
ち８０年代よりイタリア盆栽界に
て活躍する。渡日は回をかさね、
大宮で盆栽を学ぶほか、日本の主
要な盆栽展を観学する。イタリア
盆栽家連盟の創立者のひとり。

P.19
樹種：　杜松
樹高：　６５×１０２cm
素材：　山取り、１９８４年
鉢：　　常滑

P.20
樹種：　糸杉
樹高：　５１×５５cm
素材：　実生
鉢：　　常滑

P.26
樹種：　西洋ブナ
樹高：　６８×８４cm
素材：　山取り、１９８０年
鉢：　　日本

P.27
樹種：　真柏
樹高：　７８×８０cm
素材：　植木
鉢：　　常滑

P.28
樹種：　西洋一位
樹高：　４３×５２cm
素材：　山取り、１９９２年
鉢：　　韓国

P.29
樹種：　アサダ
樹高：　５５×５８cm
素材：　山取り、１９８７年
鉢：　　日本

C.LEWIS

コリン・レウィス
　　　　　　（イギリス）

１９４６年、英国に生まれる。グ
ラフィック　コンセプターの仕事
をするかたわら、２０数年前から
盆栽を愛好する。西洋の文化、芸
術から示唆を得た盆栽を創作研究
する。盆栽の指導に欧米各国を訪
れ、著書の数も多い。

P.31
樹種：　西洋落葉松
樹高：　５７×５８cm
樹齢：　１７年
素材：　実生
鉢：　　ヴァルサル　スタジオ

P.32
樹種：　西洋ニレケヤキ
樹高：　２４×２０cm
樹齢：　２３年
素材：　実生
鉢：　　ブライアン・アルブライト

P.36
樹種：　西洋ニレケヤキ
樹高：　４５×４３cm
樹齢：　１７年
素材：　実生
鉢：　　ヴァルサル　スタジオ

P.38
樹種：　西洋ニレケヤキ
樹高：　４０×４２cm
樹齢：　４０年
素材：　山取り、１９８７年
鉢：　　日本

P.39
樹種：　真柏
樹高：　６８×６５cm
素材：　はめ込み木、１９９６年
鉢：　　ブライアン・アルブライト

P.40
樹種：　西洋ニレケヤキ
樹高：　３５×４０cm
樹齢：　３０年
素材：　根
鉢：　　ゴルドン・デュフェット

P.41
樹種：　西洋はんの木
樹高：　７５×６３cm
樹齢：　１５年
素材：　実生
鉢：　　ヴァルサル　スタジオ

S.LIPORACE

サルヴァトール・リポラス
　　　　　　　　（イタリア）

イタリア生まれ。盆栽を職業とする。日本で盆栽を勉学し、イタリアのテレビ、ラジオなどで講義をする。欧米において盆栽に関する数多くの記事を書く。盆栽に対する独自の解釈をもち、ヨーロッパにおける盆栽整形の実演者の一人として著名。

P.43
樹種：　ミューゴ松
樹高：　４６cm
樹齢：　１６０年
素材：　山取り
鉢：　　中国

P.44
樹種：　サンジョゼ　ジュニパー
樹高：　５０cm
樹齢：　８０年
素材：　植木、１９８９年
鉢：　　常滑

P.50
樹種：　ピジフェラ　サワラ
樹高：　６８cm
樹齢：　６０年
素材：　植木
鉢：　　常滑

P.51
樹種：　ピセア
樹高：　６５cm
樹齢：　９０年
素材：　山取り
鉢：　　日本

P.52
樹種：　杜松
樹高：　９２cm
樹齢：　２００年
素材：　山取り
鉢：　　常滑

P.53
樹種：　西洋一位
樹高：　５３cm
樹齢：　６０年
素材：　植木
鉢：　　常滑

M.NOELANDERS

マーク・ノエランデール
　　　　　　　　（ベルギー）

１９６０年、ベルギー生まれ。日本の文化を研究するため、２１才の時７ヶ月間渡日し、そのおり盆栽に興味をもつ。その後数回、日本にて盆栽を勉強する。１９９０年より盆栽を職業とし、独創性をもった盆栽創作家として各国で実技講演をする。

P.55
樹種：　シルヴェストリス松
樹高：　６３×６１cm
樹齢：　４５年
素材：　植木、１９９６年
鉢：　　常滑

P.57
樹種：　西洋一位
樹高：　９７×９０cm
樹齢：　６０年
素材：　植木、１９９１年
鉢：　　常滑

P.62
樹種：　メタセコイヤ
樹高：　１２０×６８cm
樹齢：　４０年
素材：　植木、１９８９年
鉢：　　常滑

P.63
樹種：　ピセア
樹高：　６３×４４cm
樹齢：　３０年
素材：　植木、１９９５年
鉢：　　常滑

P.64
樹種：　ミューゴ松
樹高：　５８×８３cm
樹齢：　６０年
素材：　山取り、１９９６年
鉢：　　常滑

P.65
樹種：　杜松
樹高：　４４×４７cm
樹齢：　１６０年
素材：　山取り、１９９４年
鉢：　　常滑

P.NOTTER

ピウス・ノテール
　　　　　　　　（スイス）

１９７６年に山取り素材から盆栽を創作して以来、ヨーロッパにおいてその分野のパイオニアとされる。外国人でもっとも著名な盆栽整形の実演者として、日本の栽界から認められている。ヨーロッパ盆栽協会の設立者の一人。

P.67
樹種：　サビナビャクシン
樹高：　１２０×９０cm
素材：　山取り
鉢：　　常滑

P.68
樹種：　ピセア
樹高：　７５×７５cm
素材：　山取り、１９９４年
鉢：　　常滑

P.74
樹種：　西洋落葉松
樹高：　７５×９５cm
素材：　山取り
鉢：　　常滑

P.75
樹種：　西洋落葉松
樹高：　４０×７０cm
素材：　山取り
鉢：　　ゴルドン・デュフェット

P.76
樹種：　ミューゴ松
樹高：　７０×１００cm
素材：　山取り
鉢：　　常滑

P.77
樹種：　樫
樹高：　９０×１８０cm
素材：　山取り
鉢：　　常滑

W.PALL

ワルター・パール

（ドイツ）

１９４４年生まれ。オーストリア
で育つ。米国とオーストリアにて
経済学を学んだ後、電子部門会社
の経営をするかたわら盆栽を職業
とする。ヨーロッパ産の樹木で作
る盆栽を専門とする。１９９７年
より、ヨーロッパ盆栽協会の副会
長をつとめる。

P.79
樹種：　ピセア
樹高：　９９cm
樹齢：　１００年
素材：　山取り、１９８７年
鉢：　　デレック・アスピナル

P.80
樹種：　西洋ソロ
樹高：　８４cm
樹齢：　５０年
素材：　山取り、１９８６年
鉢：　　ブライアン・アルブライト

P.86
樹種：　ミューゴ松
樹高：　７４cm
樹齢：　１００年
素材：　山取り、１９８４年
鉢：　　ピーター・クレブス

P.87
樹種：　西洋杜松
樹高：　８２×８２cm
樹齢：　２００年
素材：　山取り、１９９４年
鉢：　　デレック・アスピナル

P.88
樹種：　ミューゴ松
樹高：　７５cm
樹齢：　１００年
素材：　山取り、１９８５年
鉢：　　デレック・アスピナル

P.89
樹種：　西洋ソロ
樹高：　６６cm
樹齢：　５０年
素材：　山取り、１９８５年
鉢：　　イキシング・ロチュス

P.RICHERT

パトリック・リシェール

（フランス）

少年期から日本とその格技に熱中
する。１９８６年より盆栽を職業
とする。盆栽の創造性を考える前
に、生きた植物としての在りかた
を重視すると云う視点に立って創
作する。消耗品的な商品盆栽から
芸術としての本格盆栽への昇華を
考える。

P.91
樹種：　ソロ
樹高：　８５×５４cm
樹齢：　６５年
原産：　日本
鉢：　　常滑

P.92
樹種：　五葉松
樹高：　１０５cm
原産：　日本、１９９４年
鉢：　　常滑

P.98
樹種：　雀梅
樹高：　５５×４５cm
樹齢：　８０年
原産：　韓国
鉢：　　韓国

P.99
樹種：　五葉松
樹高：　４５cm
原産：　日本、１９９５年
鉢：　　中国

P.100
樹種：　梅
樹高：　４５cm
原産：　日本、１９９３年
鉢：　　日本

P.101
樹種：　楓
樹高：　９５cm
原産：　日本、１９９３年
鉢：　　韓国

J.SKAMMERITZ

ヨルゲン・スカメリッツ

（デンマーク）

１０年前より盆栽を趣味とし、５
年前から職業とする。デンマーク
語で２冊の盆栽技術書を出してお
り、ヨーロッパ盆栽協会ならびに
デンマーク盆栽ソサイエティーの
メンバーで、ヴァイキングと云う
あだなで呼ばれている。今年で４
３才。

P.103
樹種：　五葉松
樹高：　４０×５０cm
樹齢：　５６年
鉢：　　ダン・バルトン

P.104
樹種：　西洋ブナ
樹高：　７０×６３cm
樹齢：　４５年
素材：　山取り、１９８９年
鉢：　　常滑

P.110
樹種：　西洋一位
樹高：　６５×４０cm
樹齢：　３７年
素材：　山取り、１９９３年
鉢：　　ヨルゲン・スカメリッツ

P.111
樹種：　ピラカンサ
樹高：　２３×２４cm
樹齢：　２５年
鉢：　　常滑

P.112
樹種：　スピノザ欅
樹高：　２３×３５cm
樹齢：　６８年
素材：　山取り、１９９４年
鉢：　　ダン・バルトン

P.113
樹種：　モチノキ
樹高：　６０×５０cm
樹齢：　５２年
素材：　植木、１９９１年
鉢：　　韓国

L.VALLEJO

ルイス・ヴァレホ
　　　　　　　　（スペイン）

１９５７年、マドリッドに生まれ
る。園芸を専攻し造園建築家とな
る。１９８５年より盆栽を教授す
る。スペイン旧総理大臣が所有す
る盆栽を管理するほか、モロッコ
国王御用達の、アトラス山脈に産
する樹木採集の任をもつ。

P.115
樹種：　サビナ真柏
樹高：　５２cm
素材：　山取り、１９９３年
鉢：　　常滑

P.116
樹種：　西洋ブナ
樹高：　５０cm
素材：　山取り、１９８８年
鉢：　　常滑

P.122
樹種：　西洋ブナ
樹高：　４８cm
素材：　山取り、１９８７年
鉢：　　ダヴィッド・ベナヴェンテ

　　マドリッド市立博物館展示

P.123
樹種：　西洋モミジ
素材：　山取り、１９９２年
鉢：　　常滑
　　マドリッド、レアル植物園

P.124
樹種：　シルヴェストリス松
樹高：　３９cm
素材：　山取り、１９８９年
鉢：　　ダヴィッド・ベナヴェンテ

P.125
樹種：　西洋ブナ
樹高：　５６cm
素材：　山取り、１９８６年
鉢：　　常滑

K.WILLSON

ケヴィン・ウィルソン
　　　　　　　　（イギリス）

１９５９年、イギリス生まれ。年
少の頃から日本の芸術、特に盆栽
に興味をもつ。山取り盆栽を中心
に創作をかさね、特に高山の樹木
を表現した盆栽を自己の作風とす
る。

P.127
樹種：　西洋ソロ
素材：　山取り、１９９２年
鉢：　　デレック・アスピナル

P.128
樹種：　西洋一位
素材：　山取り、１９８２年
鉢：　　デレック・アスピナル

P.134
樹種：　西洋一位
素材：　山取り、１９８９年
鉢：　　デレック・アスピナル

P.135
樹種：　西洋落葉松
素材：　植木、１９８４年
鉢：　　デレック・アスピナル

P.136
樹種：　西洋一位
素材：　山取り、１９８４年
鉢：　　デレック・アスピナル

P.137
樹種：　西洋一位
素材：　山取り、１９９０年
鉢：　　常滑